INTERNATIONAL DEVELOPMENT IN FOCUS

# Safe and Productive Migration from the Kyrgyz Republic

## Lessons from the COVID-19 Pandemic

LAURENT BOSSAVIE AND DANIEL GARROTE-SÁNCHEZ

**WORLD BANK GROUP**

# Contents

## Boxes

## Figures

## Tables

# Acknowledgments

This book was prepared by a team led by Laurent Bossavie (Economist, Social Protection and Jobs Global Practice, Europe and Central Asia [HECSP]) together with Daniel Garrote-Sánchez (Consultant, HECSP) and Manuel Salazar (Lead Social Protection Specialist, HECSP). It represents the main deliverable of the task "Policy Options to Address the Vulnerability of Migrants from the Kyrgyz Republic to COVID-19 and Beyond," prepared under the overall supervision of Cem Mete (Practice Manager, HECSP) and Naveed Hassan Naqvi (Country Manager for the Kyrgyz Republic).

The authors gratefully acknowledge the comments received on an earlier draft of this report by the Ministry of Labor, Social Development and Migration of the Kyrgyz Republic and by World Bank peer reviewers: Syed Amer Ahmed (Senior Economist, Social Protection and Jobs Global Practice, South Asia), Maddalena Honorati (Senior Economist, Social Protection and Jobs Global Practice, Jobs Group), and Soonhwa Yi (Senior Economist, Social Protection and Jobs Global Practice, East Asia and the Pacific). The authors would also like to thank the broader Social Protection team in the Kyrgyz Republic, in particular Chinara Ismatova (Consultant, HECSP) and Marina Novikova (Social Protection Specialist, HECSP), for continuous discussions on the topic that enriched this book. The authors are also grateful to the National Statistical Committee of the Kyrgyz Republic for sharing the microdata from their 2020 COVID-19 household survey that was used throughout this study, and to William Hutchins Seitz (Senior Economist, Poverty Global Practice, Europe and Central Asia region [ECCPV]) and Saida Ismailakhunova (Senior Economist, ECCPV) for their collaboration in designing and sharing the microdata from the survey "Listening to the Citizens of the Kyrgyz Republic." The authors would also like to thank Meerim Sagynbaeva (Consultant, Country Office of the Kyrgyz Republic) for her continuous support. Finally, the authors owe a special thank you to Cindy Fisher of the World Bank's Publishing Program for her great support, professionalism, and patience throughout the publishing process.

# About the Authors

**Laurent Bossavie** is an economist in the World Bank's Social Protection and Jobs Global Practice, Europe and Central Asia Region. His main areas of expertise are labor economics and the economics of migration. His work explores the role of labor and migration policies in shaping the labor market outcomes of workers in both advanced economies and developing countries. His research on these topics has been published in leading peer-reviewed journals in labor economics, such as the *Journal of Human Resources*, and as World Bank books and reports. He holds a PhD in economics from the European University Institute in Florence, Italy.

**Daniel Garrote-Sánchez** is a consultant in the World Bank's Social Protection and Jobs Global Practice, Europe and Central Asia Region. His areas of research include the drivers and impact of labor migration and forced displacement in sending and receiving countries, integration in host communities, and return migration. Before joining the World Bank, he worked for the Lebanese Center of Policy Studies, the Ministry of Labor of Saudi Arabia, and the Central Bank of Spain. He holds a master's degree in public administration and international development from the Harvard Kennedy School and a BA in economics and law from Carlos III University.

# Executive Summary

International migration is a critical source of employment and income for a large proportion of the Kyrgyz population. Since the 2000s, international migration has been providing job opportunities for a large number of workers from the Kyrgyz Republic and their families, in the context of a youth bulge and limited absorptive capacity of the domestic economy.[1] While domestic real wages have increased at a fast pace during the last decade, wage differentials with countries such as Kazakhstan and the Russian Federation remain large, as migrants can earn about twice the wage they would earn in the Kyrgyz Republic by working in these destinations. Under these circumstances, a large share of the Kyrgyz youth population, mostly males from rural areas, migrates overseas in search for better economic opportunities, mainly to the Russian Federation. Estimates of the total stock of Kyrgyz emigrants range from about 250,000 to 750,000 people, representing between 4 and 12 percent of the total population in the country. In 2018, prior to the COVID-19 (coronavirus) pandemic, 16 percent of households in the Kyrgyz Republic had a member currently overseas, and an even larger proportion had a member who had been overseas in the past. Among households with a current migrant, 94 percent received remittances, which represented over half (58 percent) of their total income, more than labor earnings and other sources of income combined. The Kyrgyz Republic is one of the countries with the highest dependence on international remittances worldwide: as share of the economy, remittances represented 29.2 percent of GDP in 2019, the fourth-largest recipient country in the world in relative terms (as a share of GDP), only after Tonga, Haiti, and South Sudan.

The COVID-19 pandemic, however, strongly impacted migration from the Kyrgyz Republic and exposed the limitations of current migration systems together with migrants' vulnerabilities. The primary focus of this book is on identifying the vulnerabilities and inefficiencies associated with the migration process which have been brought to light by the COVID-19 pandemic, and on policy options to reduce them and maximize the benefits of migration. While some of the challenges faced during the pandemic are specific to the COVID-19 context, many migrants' vulnerabilities already existed prior to it, and will persist in the absence of adequate policy measures. For example, COVID-19 has exposed the vulnerability of migrants to job loss in destination countries, due to limited access to social protection programs and unemployment benefits both at origin and at destination, especially among temporary or seasonal migrants. The pandemic has also exposed the need for support among migrants who return home after spending time overseas, especially among those that unexpectedly return due to shocks, such as COVID-19. Therefore, while the policy recommendations presented in this report are drawn from the COVID-19 pandemic, many of them can be implemented beyond this specific context to reduce vulnerability to external shocks—such as spillovers from the current conflict between the Russian Federation and Ukraine—and to increase the returns of migration for the Kyrgyz Republic.

The book analyzes migrants' vulnerabilities and system insufficiencies and proposes policy responses using the migration life cycle as policy framework. In contexts where temporary migration is widespread, such as the Kyrgyz Republic, the migration life cycle can typically be divided into four phases (World Bank 2018; Ahmed and Bossavie 2022): pre–migration decision, predeparture, in-service (while migrants are abroad), and return (figure ES.1). The first stage is predecision, when workers decide whether to migrate based on their understanding of the costs and benefits of migrating. The second stage is predeparture, when, after workers have decided to pursue an overseas job, they can take up measures to improve their employability (for example, undertaking additional training), look for and find a job, obtain the necessary legal documents to migrate (clearances from national authorities, visas and passports, inter alia), and complete the logistical preparations for migration (for example, tickets, financing). The third stage is during migration, when the migrant is employed overseas. The final stage is after migration, when a migrant leaves the destination to return home and, in most cases, is looking to start an economic activity in home labor markets. At each of these stages, migrants face a set of risks and inefficiencies that have been brought to light by the COVID-19 pandemic and can be mitigated by adequate policy actions.

**FIGURE ES.1**

**Migrants' decisions, COVID-19 disruptions, and policy options throughout the migration life cycle**

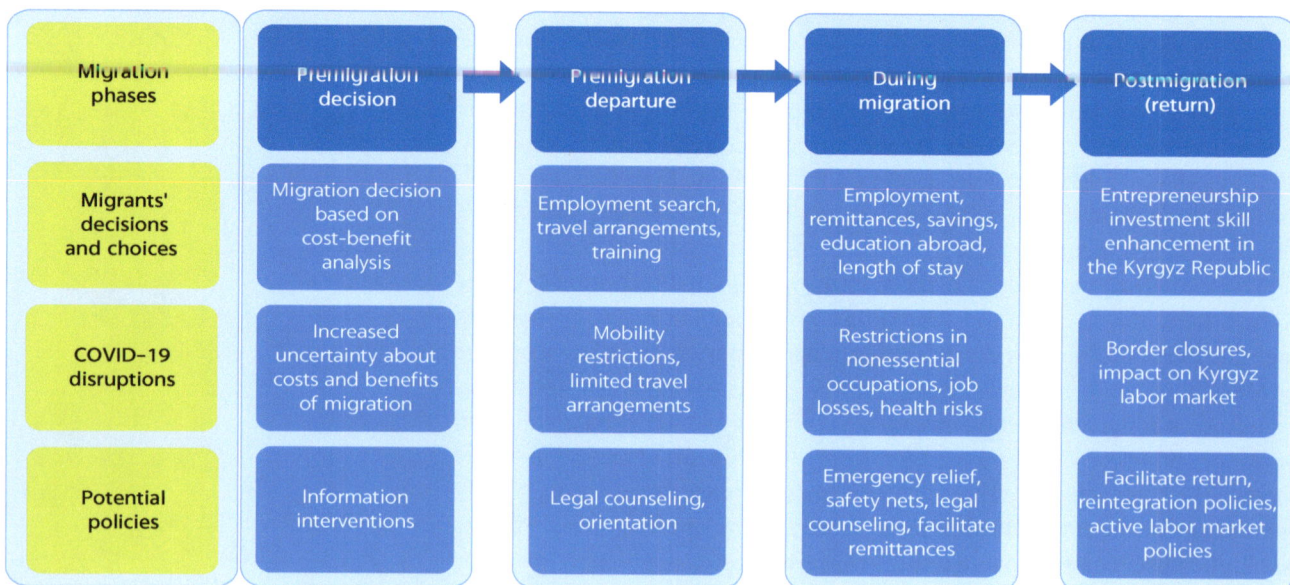

| Migration phases | Premigration decision | Premigration departure | During migration | Postmigration (return) |
|---|---|---|---|---|
| Migrants' decisions and choices | Migration decision based on cost-benefit analysis | Employment search, travel arrangements, training | Employment, remittances, savings, education abroad, length of stay | Entrepreneurship investment skill enhancement in the Kyrgyz Republic |
| COVID-19 disruptions | Increased uncertainty about costs and benefits of migration | Mobility restrictions, limited travel arrangements | Restrictions in nonessential occupations, job losses, health risks | Border closures, impact on Kyrgyz labor market |
| Potential policies | Information interventions | Legal counseling, orientation | Emergency relief, safety nets, legal counseling, facilitate remittances | Facilitate return, reintegration policies, active labor market policies |

Sources: World Bank, adapted from World Bank (2018) and Ahmed and Bossavie (2022).

The COVID-19 pandemic has led to a drastic drop in demand for migrant labor in the main destination countries, revealing the high exposure of migration flows to shocks in destination countries. In 2020, following the outbreak of the COVID-19 pandemic, the Russian Federation granted work visas to 190,000 Kyrgyz citizens, less than half of the work authorizations issued in 2019 (454,000). Compared to the same quarter in 2019, the Russian Federation approved 78,000 fewer work visas in the second quarter of 2020, 108,000 fewer in the third quarter, and 72,000 fewer in the fourth quarter (figure ES.2). That is, between March and December 2020, there were 258,000 fewer visas for Kyrgyz workers to legally work in the Russian Federation compared to the same period of 2019. These recent trends point to a drastic limitation of labor migration as a poverty alleviation tool in the Kyrgyz Republic, putting further pressure on the domestic Kyrgyz labor market. While migration from the Kyrgyz Republic picked up again in 2021, statistics from the 2021 Listening to the Citizens of the Kyrgyz Republic (L2CK) survey show that there were 167,000 temporary migrants abroad, about 40 percent fewer than prior to the pandemic.

As a result of the pandemic, many potential migrants and their households had their migration plans cancelled, placing them in a highly vulnerable situation. The survey on the impact of the COVID-19 pandemic run by the Kyrgyz National Statistics Committee in October 2020 shows a drastic disruption in emigration plans after the outbreak of the pandemic. About 9 percent of Kyrgyz households had at least one member who cancelled their travel plans abroad. Given that there are about 1.57 million households in the country, this implies that close to 150,000 households had at least one member who could not travel abroad as planned. Taking into consideration that about 250,000 Kyrgyz workers emigrate every year for a short-term period—based on the Kyrgyz Integrated Household Survey (KIHS) statistics—the number of disrupted migration plans was very large. These disruptions took place in a context where the domestic economy was also strongly hit by negative employment shocks. Furthermore, the COVID-19 survey in the Kyrgyz Republic shows that households with a member unable to migrate were twice as likely to report employment losses during the pandemic compared to those that did not have intentions to migrate (40 percent versus 19 percent) (figure ES.2). They were also more likely to report wage-income losses and needing to use harmful coping mechanisms such as cutting food spending due to lack of income. Therefore, the unexpected cancellation of migration plans associated with the pandemic appears to have placed households in a situation of acute vulnerability.

The COVID-19 pandemic showed that migrant workers from the Kyrgyz Republic are disproportionately exposed and hit by employment shocks in destination countries. Kyrgyz migrants hold jobs in occupations that are more vulnerable to the COVID-19 pandemic, and presumably to other shocks, compared to Kyrgyz nonmigrants. Panels a and b of figure ES.3 highlight several important results. In general, mid-educated workers (those who completed secondary education) are the most likely to be employed in essential occupations, while the ability to work from home increases with the level of education. When combining the two aspects of protection against COVID-19 in the labor market, higher-educated workers have a larger share of jobs that are safer from dismissal and income losses (panel c). By migration status, while 64 percent of nonmigrant workers in the Kyrgyz Republic were employed in income-safe jobs, only 46 percent of emigrants were employed in these types of jobs. Therefore, Kyrgyz emigrants are

FIGURE ES.2

## Impacts of COVID-19 on labor demand for Kyrgyz migrants and on households with disrupted migration plans, 2018–20

**a. Change in the number of visas authorized by the Russian Federation to Kyrgyz citizens (compared to the same quarter in the previous year)**

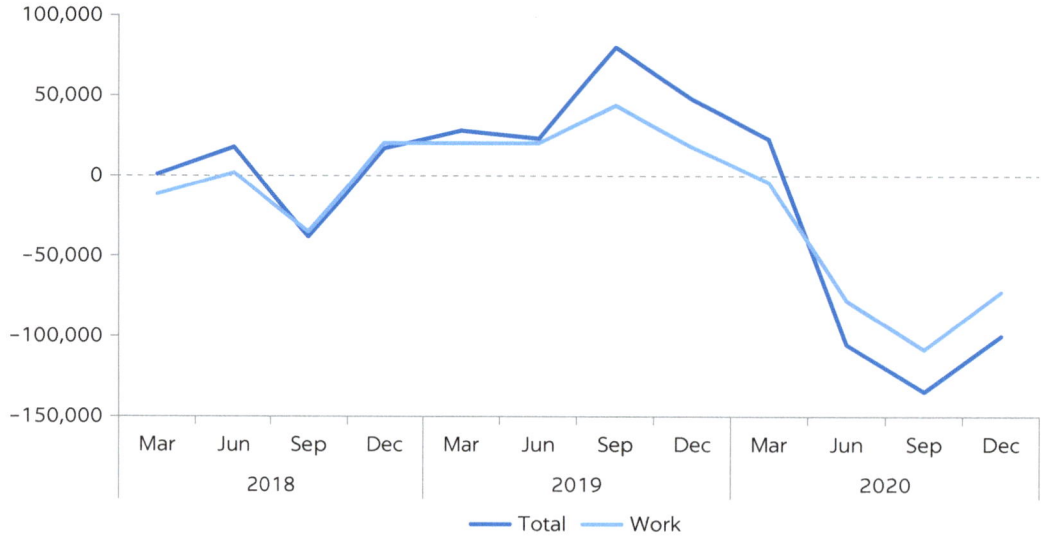

*Source:* Russian Federation Federal State Statistics Service.

**b. Impact of COVID-19 on economic and health outcomes of families with migration plans cancelled**

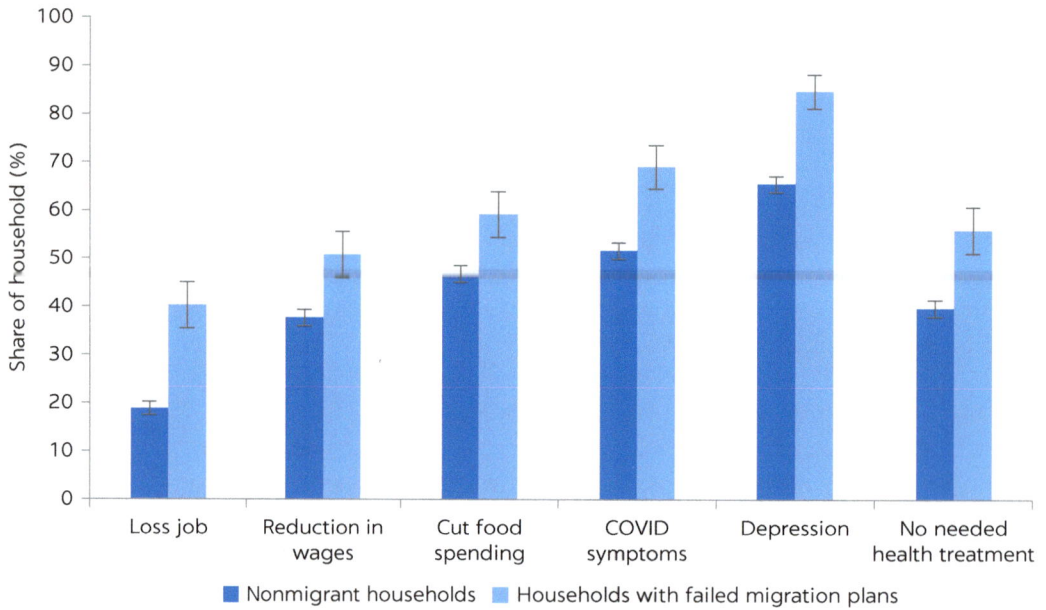

*Source:* National Statistical Committee household survey 2020.

significantly more vulnerable to supply and demand shocks to the labor market of sending countries (mainly the Russian Federation).

Surveys of migrants in the Russian Federation corroborate the larger negative impact of COVID-19 on the labor market outcomes of migrants in the first months of the pandemic, compared to both native Russians and nonmigrants in the Kyrgyz Republic. Several surveys conducted in the Russian Federation report that migrants from the Kyrgyz Republic and other Central Asian countries suffered from employment losses in the first two months of the pandemic (Varshaver, Ivanova, and Rocheva 2020; Ryazantsev and Khramova 2020; Denisenko and Mukomel 2020). About 40 percent of Kyrgyz migrants lost their jobs during the first two months of the pandemic, and an additional 39 percent

**FIGURE ES.3**

**Exposure to COVID-19 employment shocks, by migration status**

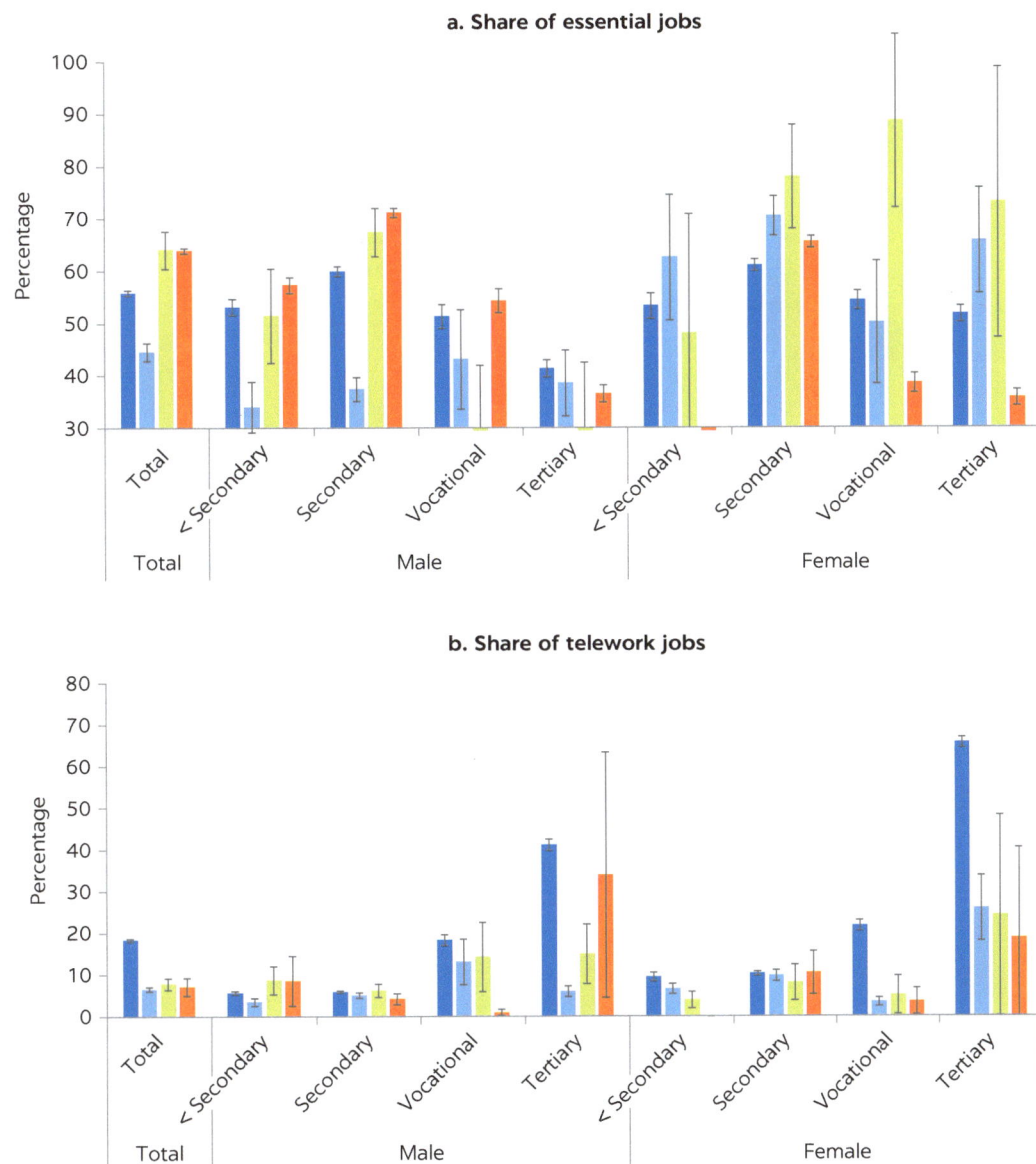

**a. Share of essential jobs**

**b. Share of telework jobs**

*continued*

FIGURE ES.3, *continued*

**c. Share of Income-safe jobs**

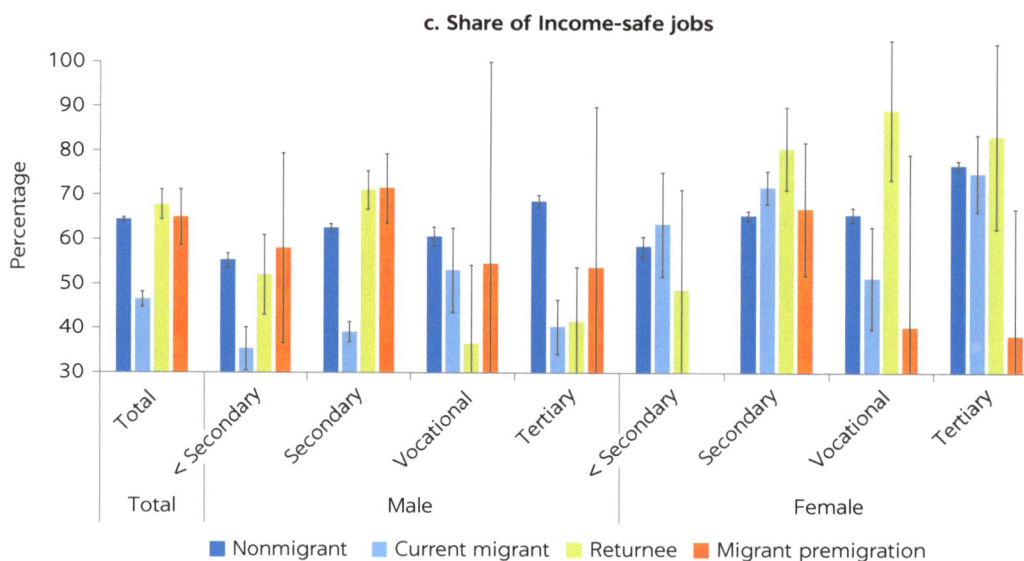

Legend: ■ Nonmigrant   ■ Current migrant   ■ Returnee   ■ Migrant premigration

*Sources:* World Bank, based on data from the 2015 Kyrgyz Integrated Household Survey and ad hoc migration module, following the methodology of Dingel and Neiman (2020), and Fasani and Mazza (2020).

were sent to unpaid leave (Varshaver, Ivanova, and Rocheva 2020). Therefore, only one in five Kyrgyz migrants was able to keep earning wages. As a comparison, about 40 percent of Russian workers were either dismissed or on unpaid leave during the same period. Other surveys of Central Asian migrants show similar results. Ryazantsev and Khramova (2020) find that 28 percent of migrants lost their job and 37 percent were on unpaid leave, and Denisenko and Mukomel (2020) observe a 30 percent drop in employment of migrants in April and May of 2020 compared to February of the same year. Across types of labor migrants, the negative shock was particularly acute among migrants with informal contracts, lower education levels, and limited Russian language fluency (Denisenko and Mukomel 2020). In consonance with the fall in employment, Varshaver, Ivanova, and Rocheva (2020) find that only 15 percent of Kyrgyz migrants maintained their levels of pre-COVID-19 labor earnings. In the second half of 2021, when the economic situation had already improved, the Listening to the Citizens of the Kyrgyz Republic (L2CK) survey shows that 64 percent of Kyrgyz migrants in the Russian Federation were employed, still significantly lower rates than premigration when temporary migrants were almost universally employed.

Kyrgyz migrants not only experienced dramatic job losses, but they also had limited access to social protection programs to weather the COVID-19 shock. Kyrgyz labor migrants usually fall through the cracks of social protection systems in both receiving countries and at home. In the Kyrgyz Republic, spending on social protection is similar to other benchmark countries in the region. However, labor migrants are unable to contribute to the Kyrgyz social insurance system, which poses a longer-term threat to the fiscal sustainability of the Kyrgyz pension systems (OECD 2018). In host countries, even within the Eurasian Economic Union (EaEU), Kyrgyz emigrants do not have access to services such as health care or unemployment benefits as natives do (Sharifzoda 2019). As the 2018 KIHS shows, only 13 percent of Kyrgyz workers abroad have access to social security benefits (figure ES.4). Overall, Kyrgyz migrant workers have

**FIGURE ES.4**

## Type of contract and legal protection of Kyrgyz emigrants and nonmigrants

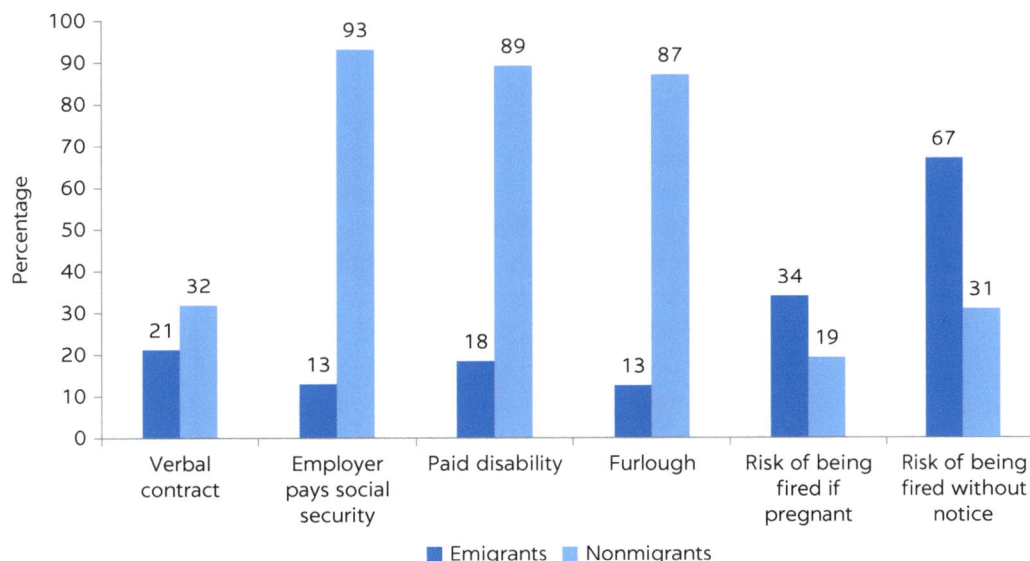

*Source:* Kyrgyz Republic Integrated Household Survey (2018).

very limited access to social protection programs either in their own country or abroad, which makes them and their families particularly vulnerable to negative income or health shocks that could push them into poverty. Given the status quo of informality and limited social protection, many migrants working abroad lost their jobs without receiving any compensation or protection (Kuznetsova et al. 2020). In the event of contracting the virus, Kyrgyz emigrants also lacked proper access to health care and were more exposed to layoffs if they required a sickness leave. The lack of social protection of Kyrgyz migrants has had dramatic consequences during the pandemic, with a vast majority struggling to obtain enough funding to pay basic expenditures such as rent and food (Ryazantsev and Khramova 2020).

The labor market reintegration of returnees resulting from the COVID-19 pandemic has been challenging given the limited absorptive capacity of the Kyrgyz labor market. In addition to disrupting the migration plans of prospective migrants, the pandemic has led to the unexpected return of some migrants who were already overseas. According to the L2CK survey, more than 78,000 migrants returned to the Kyrgyz Republic between March 2020 and October 2021. When surveying migrants from Central Asia that returned home from the Russian Federation after the COVID-19 outbreak, Denisenko and Mukomel (2020) found that only 40 percent of them were employed by early June 2020. The 2020 National Statistics Committee COVID-19 survey also shows a higher degree of economic and health vulnerability of households with members that were either forced to return or were stranded and could not return from abroad. While less than 20 percent of nonmigrant households reported having members who lost their job during the pandemic, the rate reached 33 percent for households with a migrant that could not return and was stranded, and 54 percent for households with a member that had to return to the Kyrgyz Republic. Households with recent returnees not only were more likely than nonmigrant families to see a reduction in wage income since the start of the pandemic, but also in remittances which, as chapter 1 shows, represent an increasing share of income for migrant families. Given the larger negative shock that families with returnees faced, they were also significantly more likely to report using strategies such as cutting food spending to cope with lower incomes. Healthwise, households with recent returnees also had a higher incidence of COVID-19-related symptoms and mental health issues, and were more likely to be left without the necessary health treatment.

Overall, the COVID-19 pandemic highlighted the need to strengthen institutions, frameworks, and data collection to enhance safe legal migration from the Kyrgyz Republic. The existing migration management in the Kyrgyz Republic is still lacking a centralized data system and intersectoral collaboration throughout the migration cycle—from migration plans and preparations, to support and protection during the migration experience, to the reintegration of returning labor migrants in the Kyrgyz Republic. Migration policy has to be informed by relevant and updated data, beyond aggregate statistics of border crossings for security purposes and remittances data, in order to elaborate effective mechanisms to support migrants and their families (Kuznetsova et al. 2020). Legal frameworks have yet to be developed and implemented to put at the forefront of the migration agenda a rights-based approach to protect migrants and their families. In the absence of a holistic migration framework with predictable policies, programs to support migrants coping with the COVID-19 crisis have been fragmented and of limited scope.

Enhancing systematic data collection, monitoring, and evaluation throughout the migration life cycle is necessary in a context of sizable flows of emigrants and returnees to better understand migration dynamics and tailor services to migrants' needs. As a first step, it is necessary to centralize information from different governmental bodies—which requires interagency cooperation and data sharing—and to create a unified registry of all prospective migrants, current migrants, and returnees, either at reception centers or at different points of exit or entry in the country. The registry can serve as the starting point to collect data on the skills and labor market situation of Kyrgyz citizens applying for jobs overseas—so they can be referred to the appropriate training or premigration programs. The registry can also be a building block in the reintegration of returnees and to create monitoring systems through the adoption of harmonized sets of indicators (IOM 2018). Different agencies could then more easily access migrants' information, avoiding duplicity of procedures and overburdening migrant returnees, while collecting higher-quality information to tailor services to their needs. It is essential that this process of data sharing and cooperation complies with the need to maintain migrants' privacy.

Policies to address the vulnerability of migrants in the context of the COVID-19 pandemic and in the longer term need to tackle challenges throughout the migration life cycle. The COVID-19 pandemic has impacted prospective and current migrants at each stage of the migration life cycle. This book proposes a set of policies that can be implemented at the predeparture, during-migration, and after-return stages to reduce the vulnerability of migrants in the context of the COVID-19 pandemic and beyond. Given the expected slow recovery from COVID-19, both at home and in destination countries, combined with the current economic situation in the Russian Federation, the enhanced challenges faced by temporary migrants in the specific context of the pandemic are expected to persist in the short and medium runs. This challenging context can be used as an opportunity to strengthen the migration system and develop policies and programs that can equip the Kyrgyz Republic with the adequate tools to support migrants—through a coherent and comprehensive labor migration policy—and to be better prepared for future shocks that may affect labor migration and remittances.

COVID-19, and now the economic downturn in the Russian Federation, have also evidenced the need for diversification of destinations to reduce volatility. The Kyrgyz Republic has one of the largest concentrations of emigrants in the world. Close to 80 percent of total Kyrgyz emigrants in 2019 resided in the Russian Federation according to UN-DESA, and statistics for short-term migrants show an even higher proportion (over 90 percent, according to the Kyrgyz Integrated Household Survey or the 2021 Listening to the Citizens of the Kyrgyz Republic survey). The business cycle of the second main destination of Kyrgyz migrants, Kazakhstan, is highly synchronized with the Russian Federation (Jenish 2013), given their economic integration and dependence on raw materials. The high concentration of Kyrgyz migrants in few and synchronized markets exposes the country to high volatility and vulnerability to economic shocks in destination countries. COVID-19, and now the economic crisis in the Russian Federation, have shown that, as a result of this lack of diversification, migration and remittance flows are quite volatile, resulting in significant welfare losses for Kyrgyz households and for the broader economy.

To reduce the volatility of migration demand and flows, new institutional frameworks such as bilateral labor agreements (BLAs), government-to-government (G2G) arrangements, and memoranda of understanding could be implemented.[2] Such arrangements could be put in place with other destination countries with a potential demand for foreign labor given their demographic trends or labor needs (for example, in Europe, the Gulf Cooperation Council, the Republic of Korea, or Malaysia). For example, the Philippines, a country with a long tradition of emigration and with a well-developed migration system, has diversified the destination countries over the years by being very active in negotiating new bilateral labor agreements and by building a qualified workforce with credible credentials (Testaverde et al. 2017). In additional to new destinations, migration diversification can also be enhanced in terms of occupations. About half of Kyrgyz male migrants work in construction and half of female migrants in the hospitality sector. This concentration increases vulnerability to shocks in host economies that affect particular sectors. While the EaEU allows Kyrgyz migrants in the Russian Federation and Kazakhstan to work in all sectors, further cooperation might be needed with these countries to fully recognize foreign credentials. This, combined with the provision of information to migrants on the types of job opportunities available in destination countries and the provision of training to prospective migrants when skill mismatches emerge with what firms demand at destination can expand the employment opportunities available across sectors and professions.

Training for migrants driven by identified demand for skills in destination countries is key to complement this diversification effort, and address skill mismatches between demand and supply of foreign labor in existing destinations. Migrants from the Kyrgyz Republic often lack adequate skills for the jobs most in demand in the Russian Federation or Kazakhstan. Skill mismatches are partly due to occupational mobility upon migration. For example, a large portion of male migrants have an agricultural background but are hired as construction workers in the Russian Federation. Skill mismatches might have been aggravated in the context of the COVID-19 pandemic, which could have accelerated a longer-term shift in tasks and skills demanded in host labor markets. In this context, training in the skills required for employment openings in the Russian Federation would benefit all parties involved. However, prior to the pandemic, the Kyrgyz Household Integrated Survey of 2018 shows that only 1 percent of prospective migrants took any work-related training courses to improve their chances to find employment overseas. The Ministry of Labor, Social Development and Migration is planning to implement several initiatives within the recently created Fund for Skill Development. Past experiences with predeparture skill upgrading programs highlight the need to have a well-endowed program, a previous analysis of the supply and demand skill gaps and dynamics in the destination country and at origin in order to tailor the training to the most demanded skills that migrants do not possess (IOM 2011; Global Forum on Migration and Development 2020). Cooperation with receiving countries in understanding skill gaps at destination is, thus, of high value. A particularly promising type of cross-country collaboration on skill formation are global skill partnerships.

The COVID-19 pandemic highlighted the need for better integrating migrants into safety net programs either at origin or at destination to reduce migrants' vulnerabilities to shocks like COVID-19. In the Russian Federation, the government increased the amount of unemployment benefits,[3] and agreed to provide social services for citizens who lost their job after March 1, 2020, as well as to families with children and pensioners (Gorlin et al. 2020).[4] The Kyrgyz Republic could coordinate with the Russian Federation and other migrant-receiving countries, in particular within the framework of the EaEU, to provide financial support to its citizens stranded abroad and, more broadly, to create a system where migrant workers make contributions to have equal access to unemployment benefits and health care as nationals from the countries of residency. Increasing formal employment channels will improve access to social protection systems (as the concept for migration policies for 2021–30 suggests), but specific arrangements need to be implemented beyond the legal status of employment as currently even migrants with a legal contract barely have any social protection. The portability of pensions has been shown to not only enhance migrants' welfare but also to incentivize migrants to return home.

COVID-19 also evidenced the need for shock-resilient migration systems. The pandemic has been one large shock that significantly disrupted mobility globally, including from the Kyrgyz Republic. Some of the lessons learned from the pandemic, however, can also be applied to respond to other shocks, including the negative spillovers of the Russia-Ukraine conflict. This large negative shock affecting the Russian Federation, although different in nature from the COVID-19 pandemic, is having similar consequences for migrant households given the limited ability of current systems to respond to shocks. This translates into a drop in demand for migrants from the Kyrgyz Republic, a drop in remittance volumes and values, reduced emigration flows, and possibly increased returns. In the absence of measures to strengthen the responsiveness of migration systems to shocks, other future shocks—such as climate change, new health threats, or additional conflicts—are expected to have similar impacts on migrants from the Kyrgyz Republic and their families. In shock-responsive mobility systems, underlying components ranging from admission channels to provision of different types of services in receiving and sending countries are built with the flexibility to adapt to shocks. These systems require coordination between sending and receiving countries to take actions at different stages of the migration life cycle when unexpected shocks hit (Pavillion and Testaverde 2022). Before ensuring responsiveness, however, underlying migration systems, as described in the previous paragraphs, need to be in place.

The pandemic has also shown that better linkages of return migrants to active labor market policies (ALMPs) are required to support reintegration into home labor markets. While there have been recent legislative and institutional improvements, the variety and reach of ALMPs in the Kyrgyz Republic remain limited. The main ALMPs include public works and small training programs to vulnerable groups, while few resources exist for other programs for entrepreneurship and self-employment, wage subsidies, and job counseling, among others.[5] Overall, these programs are underfunded and use a rather restrictive definition of beneficiaries—as, for example, farmers with land plots exceeding 0.05 hectares are considered employed and thus ineligible (Gassmann and Timár 2018).[6] Given the higher prevalence of return migrants in rural areas and the high share that used to work as farmers before migration and engage again in agricultural work upon return—close to half of male return migrants, according to the KIHS 2015— this policy can de facto limit the ability of return migrants to access ALMPs. The public employment services (PES) provide free training for registered, unemployed individuals. However, similarly to unemployment benefits, registration is low, and PES tend to be located and register vacancies in urban areas (Schwegler-Rohmeis, Mummert, and Jarck 2013). As a result, return migrants are very unlikely to use those services.

## NOTES

1. Job creation in the country has not been able to provide enough opportunities for the rapidly expanding number of new, young entrants to the labor market as a consequence of the demographic youth bulge. While the working age population increased an average of 2 percent between 2003 and 2013, employment growth only did so at 0.9 percent (Ajwad and Berger-Gonzalez 2018).
2. For more detail on the G2G between Korea and sending countries, for example, see Cho et al. (2018).
3. Decree No. 8446 of the Government of the Russian Federation, June 10, 2020.
4. Resolution No. 4855 of the Government of the Russian Federation, April 12, 2020.
5. The public works program offers employment by public and private employers with wages partially covered by the Ministry of Labor, Social Development and Migration (MLSDM). In 2016, 21,100 people benefited from this program, with an average monthly wage of KGS 1,000-1,5000 (Gassmann and Timár 2018).
6. In 2017, only 1.2 percent of the MLSDM budget was reserved for ALMP (Gassmann and Timár 2018).

## REFERENCES

Ahmed, S. A., and L. Bossavie. 2022. "Towards Safer and More Productive Migration for South Asia." World Bank, Washington, DC. https://openknowledge.worldbank.org/handle /10986/37444.

Ajwad, M. I., and Sarah Berger-Gonzalez. 2018. "Jobs in the Kyrgyz Republic. World Bank, Washington, DC. https://openknowledge.worldbank.org/handle/10986/30105.

Cho, Y., A. Denisova, S. Yi, and U. Khadka. 2018. *Bilateral Arrangement of Temporary Labor Migration: Lessons from Korea's Employment Permit System*. Washington, DC: World Bank.

Denisenko, M., and V. Mukomel. 2020. "Labor Migration During the Corona Crisis." Institute of Demography and the Institute of Sociology FSRC RAS, June.

Dingel, J., and B. Neiman. 2020. "How Many Jobs Can Be Done at Home?" *Journal of Public Economics* 189 (September): 104235.

Fasani, F., and J. Mazza. 2020. "Immigrant Key Workers: Their Contribution to Europe's COVID-19 Response." IZA Policy Paper 155.

Gassmann, F., and E. Timár. 2018. "Scoping Study on Social Protection and Safety Nets for Enhanced Food Security and Nutrition in the Kyrgyz Republic." World Food Programme, United Nations University, and Maastricht University.

Global Forum on Migration and Development. 2020. "The Future of Human Mobility: Innovative Partnerships for Sustainable Development—Theme 2: Skilling Migrants for Employment." Abu Dhabi, United Arab Emirates.

Gorlin, Y., V. Lyashok, D. Ternovskiy, A. Bozhechkova, P. Trunin, S. Zubov, A. Kaukin, and E. Miller. 2020. "Monitoring the Economic Situation in Russia: Trends and Challenges of Socio-Economic Development." Institute for Economic Policy, Russian akademyma of the National Economy and Public Service under the President of the Russian Federation.

IOM (International Organization for Migration). 2011. "IOM Migrant Training Programmes Overview, 2010–2011." http://www.iom.int/jahia/webdav/shared/shared/mainsite /activities/facilitating/IOM_Migrant_Training_Programmes_Overview_2010_2011.pdf.

IOM (International Organization for Migration). 2018. "Supporting Safe, Orderly and Dignified Migration Through Assisted Voluntary Return and Reintegration." Global Compact Thematic Paper, Assisted Voluntary Return and Reintegration.

Jenish, N. 2013. "Business Cycles in Central Asia and the Russian Federation." University of Central Asia, Institute of Public Policy and Administration Working Paper 15.

Kuznetsova, I, R. Mogilevskii, A. Murzakulova, A. Abdoubaetova, A. Wolters, and J. Round. 2020. "Migration and COVID-19: Challenges and Policy Responses in the Kyrgyz Republic." CAP Paper 247 (December), Central Asia Program.

Kyrgyz National Statistical Committee. 2020. "The Impact of the COVID-19 Pandemic on Households." Government of the Kyrgyz Republic.

OECD (Organisation for Economic Co-operation and Development). 2018. "Social Protection System Review of Kyrgyzstan." OECD Development Pathways, OECD Publishing, Paris.

Pavillion, J., and M. Testaverde. 2022. "COVID-19 and Migration in the Mediterranean Region." Washington, DC, World Bank.

Testaverde, M., H. Moroz, C. H. Hollweg, and A. Schmillen. 2017. "Migrating to Opportunity: Overcoming Barriers to Labor Mobility in Southeast Asia." World Bank, Washington, DC. https://openknowledge.worldbank.org/handle/10986/28342.

Ryazantsev, S., and M. Khramova. 2020. "Influence of the COVID-19 Pandemic on the Position of Migrants and Remittances in Central Asia." Institute for Socio-Political Research of the Russian Academy of Sciences.

Schwegler-Rohmeis, W., A. Mummert, and K. Jarck. 2013. "Labour Market and Employment Policy in the Kyrgyz Republic: Identifying Constraints and Options for Employment Development." Deutsche Gesellschaft für Internationale Zusammenarbeit GmbH, Eschborn/Bishkek.

Sharifzoda, K. 2019. "Central Asia's Russian Migration Puzzle: An interview with Caress Schenk." *The Diplomat,* October 11. https://thediplomat.com/2019/10/central -asias-russian-migration-puzzle.

Testaverde, M., H. Moroz, C. H. Hollweg, and A. Schmillen. 2017. "Migrating to Opportunity: Overcoming Barriers to Labor Mobility in Southeast Asia." World Bank, Washington, DC. https://openknowledge.worldbank.org/handle/10986/28342.

Varshaver, E., N. Ivanova, and A. Rocheva. 2020. "Migrants in Russia during the COVID-19 Pandemic: Survey Results." *RANEPA 2020* [in Russian]. https://papers.ssrn.com/sol3 /papers.cfm?abstract_id=3672397.

World Bank. 2018. "A Migrant's Journey for Better Opportunities: The Case of Pakistan." World Bank, Washington, DC. https://openknowledge.worldbank.org/handle/10986/30272.

# Abbreviations

| | |
|---|---|
| ALMP | active labor market policies |
| EaEU | Eurasian Economic Union |
| G2G | government-to-government arrangements |
| GDP | gross domestic product |
| ILO | International Labour Organization |
| IMF | International Monetary Fund |
| IOM | International Organization for Migration |
| KIHS | Kyrgyz Integrated Household Survey |
| L2CK | Listening to the Citizens of the Kyrgyz Republic (survey) |
| MLSDM | Ministry of Labor, Social Development and Migration |
| NGO | nongovernmental organization |
| OECD | Organisation for Economic Co-operation and Development |
| PES | public employment services |
| SMS | State Migration Services |
| UN-DESA | United Nations Department of Economic and Social Affairs |
| UNICEF | United Nations Children's Fund |

# Introduction

Over the last two decades, international migration has been an essential employment and income-generating strategy for many households in the Kyrgyz Republic given the limited absorptive capacity of the local labor market. Since the 2000s, job creation in the country has not been able to provide enough opportunities to the rapidly expanding number of new, young entrants to the labor market as a consequence of the demographic youth bulge. While the working age population increased an average of 2 percent between 2003 and 2013, employment growth only did so at 0.9 percent (Ajwad and Berger-Gonzalez 2018). Beyond job availability, the quality of employment has remained low, with high degrees of informality, seasonality, and lack of tenure (World Bank 2015). While real wages have increased at a fast pace during the last decade, wage differentials remain large compared to countries such as Kazakhstan and the Russian Federation. Under these circumstances, many Kyrgyz youth, in particular males from rural areas, migrate overseas in search of better economic opportunities, in particular to the Russian Federation. Estimates of the total stock of Kyrgyz emigrants range from about 250,000 to 750,000 people, representing between 4 and 12 of the total population in the country. While international labor migration in the Kyrgyz Republic alleviates labor market pressures and supports domestic income and consumption of migrant households through remittances, it also produces certain vulnerabilities for migrants given the high concentration geographically—mostly to the Russian Federation—and in very specific sectors and occupations and limited social protection coverage. Migrant families and the country as a whole are also more exposed to shocks to remittances.

The COVID-19 pandemic, has produced dramatic health and economic costs, disrupting the Kyrgyz economy and the labor mobility of Kyrgyz migrants. The spread of the COVID-19 pandemic in the Kyrgyz Republic caused more than 100,000 diagnosed cases and 1,700 deaths by May 2021.[1] The economic activity was severely affected by mobility restrictions, the increase in uncertainty and lower demand. According to the International Monetary Fund (IMF) estimates of April 2021, the Kyrgyz GDP fell by

8 percent in real terms, the largest drop since 1994. In the domestic labor market, the Kyrgyz National Statistics Committee COVID-19 survey reports that about one in five households in the country had a family member that lost their job in the first months of the pandemic. In this context, international migration from the Kyrgyz Republic has also been severely impacted. Mobility disruptions, border closures, and limited travel options have limited the ability of many prospective migrants to move overseas in search of better employment opportunities. Kyrgyz migrants who were living abroad at the time the pandemic hit have been particularly exposed to the large economic shock in destination countries, as the occupations they work in are less likely to be amenable to work from home. This resulted in large declines in employment and earnings (Varshaver, Ivanova, and Rocheva 2020; Ryazantsev and Khramova 2020; Denisenko and Mukomel 2020). With travel restrictions, many migrants were stranded without the option to return home and with a lack of social protection mechanisms.

COVID-19 has put migrants' vulnerabilities at the forefront, but many of those existed prior to the pandemic, and they will continue to exist if adequate policies are not put in place. The primary focus of this book is on the vulnerability of migrants in the specific context of COVID-19, and on policy options to mitigate the negative impacts on labor migrants, who have been disproportionately affected. While some of the challenges faced during the pandemic are specific to the COVID-19 context, many of migrants' vulnerabilities already existed but were made more salient by the pandemic. For example, COVID-19 has exposed the vulnerability of migrants to job loss in destination, due to limited access to social protection programs and employment benefits both at origin and at destination, especially among temporary or seasonal migrants. The pandemic has also exposed the need for support among migrants who returned home after spending time overseas, especially among those that returned unexpectedly due to shocks. Therefore, while the book recommends policy actions to address migrants' vulnerability in the specific context of the pandemic, it also proposes policies that can be implemented to reduce vulnerability more broadly, beyond the specific context of COVID-19.

This book takes stock of the patterns, vulnerabilities, and inefficiencies of international labor migration from the Kyrgyz Republic, with a particular focus on the recent impact of the COVID-19 pandemic on migration flows, migrants, and their families. It provides policy recommendations to enhance the benefits of safe international migration and address migrants' vulnerabilities in the context of the COVID-19 pandemic and beyond. The scope of the book is limited to international labor migration. It does not cover mobility within the country, as well as refugees and the resettlement of ethnic Kyrgyz (Kairylmans), as the set of policy issues is quite distinct and would require a separate analysis and data collection. The book is structured as follows. Chapter 1 provides a comprehensive analysis of the trends and profile of migrants from the Kyrgyz Republic in the run-up to the COVID pandemic, highlighting the important role of migration and remittances for migrants and their families but also the vulnerabilities and risks associated with them. Chapter 2 assesses the vulnerability of migrants to the COVID-19 pandemic at each stage of the migration life cycle: before migration, during migration, and post migration. Chapter 3 provides policy recommendations to address the vulnerability of migrants and their families in the context of the COVID-19 pandemic and beyond.

## NOTE

1. Based on the COVID-19 Data Repository by the Center for Systems Science and Engineering (CSSE) at Johns Hopkins University. https://github.com/CSSEGISandData/COVID-19.

## REFERENCES

Ajwad, M. I., and Sarah Berger-Gonzalez. 2018. "Jobs in the Kyrgyz Republic. World Bank, Washington, DC. https://openknowledge.worldbank.org/handle/10986/30105.

Denisenko, M., and V. Mukomel. 2020. "Labor Migration During the Corona Crisis." Institute of Demography and the Institute of Sociology FSRC RAS.

Ryazantsev, S., and M. Khramova. 2020. "Influence of the COVID-19 Pandemic on the Position of Migrants and Remittances in Central Asia," Institute for Socio-Political Research of the Russian Academy of Sciences.

Varshaver, E., N. Ivanova, and A. Rocheva. 2020. "Migrants in Russia during the COVID-19 Pandemic: Survey Results." *RANEPA 2020* [in Russian]. https://papers.ssrn.com/sol3/papers.cfm?abstract_id=3672397.

World Bank. 2015. "Labor Migration and Welfare in the Kyrgyz Republic (2008–2013)." Report 99771-KG, Poverty Global Practice Europe and Central Asia Region, World Bank, Washington, DC. https://openknowledge.worldbank.org/handle/10986/22960?locale-attribute=es.

# 1 Labor Migration as a Major Source of Employment and Development

## CHARACTERISTICS OF LABOR MIGRATION FROM THE KYRGYZ REPUBLIC

Despite current data limitations in capturing migration from the Kyrgyz Republic, available data indicate that emigration from the Kyrgyz Republic is widespread (see box 1.1). There are currently no centralized administrative data that capture the full extent of labor migration from the country. Only the State Border Services have a registry of all Kyrgyz citizens and foreigners that enter and leave the country, but without clear distinction of the purpose of the travel, be it tourism, education, labor, or other. The lack of specific registry of labor migrants can be understood in a context of increasing free mobility of Kyrgyz nationals to the Russian Federation and Kazakhstan, the two main destination countries that are part of the Eurasian Economic Union, and the limited services provided by the Kyrgyz government for prospective and current migrants, as opposed to other migrant-sending countries with more mature systems, such as the Philippines. Available estimates from other sources, however, indicate that labor migration from the country is widespread. Estimates from the United Nations Department of Economic and Social Affairs (UN-DESA) migration database report that about 750,000 Kyrgyz citizens lived abroad in 2019.

Migration from the Kyrgyz Republic is heavily concentrated in one destination country. By country of residence, the broad definition of Kyrgyz emigrants by UN-DESA statistics shows that close to 80 percent reside in the Russian Federation (slightly below 600,000 people), followed by 10 percent in Germany (around 77,000, which are mostly ethnic Germans that migrated in the 1990s, taking advantage of the German nationality law that granted citizenship to anyone with proof of German ancestry) and 4 percent in Ukraine (about 27,000). The geographical composition of short-term/temporary migrants found in surveys in the Kyrgyz Republic, such as the Kyrgyz Integrated Household Survey (KIHS) or the Listening to the Citizens of the Kyrgyz Republic survey, is even more concentrated, with about 95 percent working in the Russian Federation (table 1.1).[1] Several reasons explain the predominance

BOX 1.1

## Current data limitations in measuring migration flows and stocks from the Kyrgyz Republic

Statistics on migration in the Kyrgyz Republic, as in many other migrant-sending countries, only partially capture emigration from the country. There are currently no centralized administrative data that capture the full extent of labor migration from the country. Instead, one has to rely on existing nationally representative surveys, which have their own limitations. The Kyrgyz Integrated Household Survey (KIHS) collects quarterly information on the labor market in the Kyrgyz Republic. It also collects information on the current place and country of work of all individuals in the household. This allows approximating the extent of short-term and circular migration. Through that survey question, both migrants currently working abroad (but officially residing in the Kyrgyz Republic) and seasonal migrants who currently live in the Kyrgyz Republic but spend several months of the year abroad are included. However, the survey does not capture longer-term migration, as it does not collect information on migrants who leave the household for a long period of time—even if they receive remittances from them—or entire households that leave the country (World Bank

2015). The KIHS's underestimation of migrants is also partly explained by the fact that it only focuses on labor migration, so Kyrgyz citizens who left the country for other purposes such as education are not included (Dubashov, Kruse, and Ismailakhunova 2017). Estimates of the size of emigration based on surveys in the Kyrgyz Republic only account for one-third of the numbers based on data from receiving countries. Given the restrictive definition of short-term migration used in the KIHS, the actual size of the Kyrgyz diaspora residing overseas is underestimated. In 2018, there were an estimated 250,000 working-age Kyrgyz working abroad according to the KIHS.

Aggregate information on migration flows also provides a partial picture of the migration phenomenon in the country. While migration stocks account for the number of migrants living abroad at a given point in time, migration flows report the number of migrants entering or leaving a country during a specific period of time. Mathematically, the change in the stock of emigrants in a given year is equal to the migration outflows minus the migration inflows in the same period. Official statistics from the National

FIGURE B1.1.1

**Trends in migration flows from and to the Kyrgyz Republic, 2012–20**

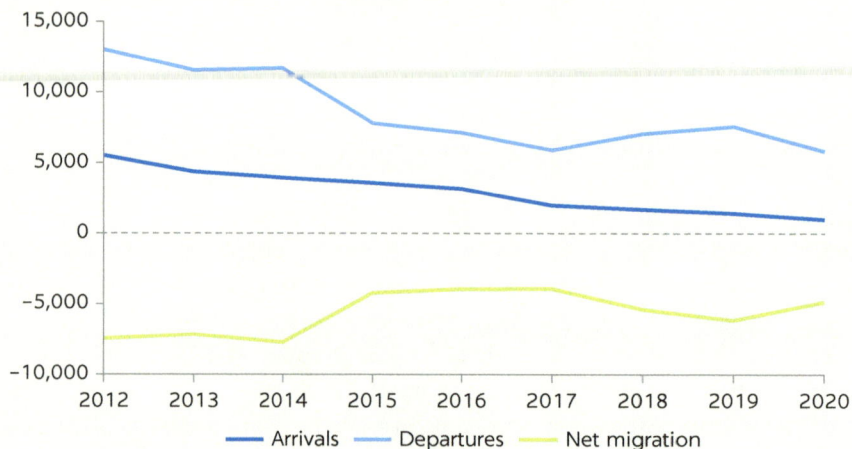

Source: Kyrgyz Republic National Statistical Committee.
Note: Net emigration is calculated as the difference between arrivals to and departures from the Kyrgyz Republic.

continued

**Box 1.1,** *continued*

Statistical Committee, however, report a reduced number of migrants leaving or returning to the country every year, significantly lower than the estimates from the Kyrgyz Integrated Household Survey (figure B1.1.1). Both departures and arrivals show a declining trend during the last decade, with numbers in both cases below 10,000 people. While these statistics still show that, on net, more people leave the country than return, thus increasing the stock of the Kyrgyz diaspora, the statistics are downward biased as they are restricted to individuals who officially register a change in residency, which is only a small fraction of the total migrant population.

TABLE 1.1  **Estimates of the stock of migrants from the Kyrgyz Republic**

| COUNTRY | LIVE ABROAD (UN-DESA, 2019) | | WORK ABROAD (KIHS, 2018) | | WORK ABROAD (L2CK, 2021) | |
|---|---|---|---|---|---|---|
| Total | 754,969 | 100% | 251,874 | 100% | 166,695 | 100% |
| Russian Federation | 591,211 | 78% | 242,608 | 96% | 157,360 | 94% |
| Germany | 77,373 | 10% | 0 | 0% | 291 | 0% |
| Ukraine | 26,996 | 4% | 0 | 0% | 0 | 0% |
| Tajikistan | 11,261 | 1% | 0 | 0% | 0 | 0% |
| Kazakhstan | 7,036 | 1% | 1,995 | 1% | 4,035 | 2% |
| United States | 6,607 | 1% | 0 | 0% | 195 | 0% |
| Other | 34,485 | 5% | 7,271 | 3% | 4,815 | 3% |

*Sources:* UN-DESA (2019), Kyrgyz Integrated Household Survey (2018), and Listening to the Citizens of the Kyrgyz Republic (2021).
*Note:* UN-DESA = United Nations Department of Economic and Social Affairs; KIHS = Kyrgyz Integrated Household Survey; L2CK = Listening to the Citizens of the Kyrgyz Republic survey.

of the Russian Federation as a destination country in the past decades—including the visa-free system, solid migrant networks, low transportation costs, and Kyrgyz workers' knowledge of the Russian language—all of which contribute to reducing migration costs.

Migration from the Kyrgyz Republic has a strong seasonal component characterized by a peak during the warmer months and a reduction due to the partial return of migrants to the Kyrgyz Republic during the winter, when the economic activity of seasonal sectors such as construction, agriculture, or tourism is lower (figure 1.1). Looking at longer-term trends, there was a rapid increase in emigration between 2005 and 2009, reaching about 250,000 workers. However, these trends reverted during the financial crisis that severely affected the price of commodities and the Russian economy. Since 2015, the number of Kyrgyz emigrants has started to increase again, reaching 250,000 by 2018. During the 2004–2018 period, migration flows from the Kyrgyz Republic and different indicators of the dynamism of the Russian economy, such as the GDP or the price of gas, show a drastically high correlation (about 0.8), proving the sensitivity of migration to fluctuations and shocks affecting the Russian economy (table 1.2).

In terms of incidence in the population of the Kyrgyz Republic, workers overseas currently represent about 6 percent of the total working age population and more than 10 percent of all employed Kyrgyz people, which shows the large

FIGURE 1.1
**Trends in the stock of temporary migrants from the Kyrgyz Republic, 2004–18**

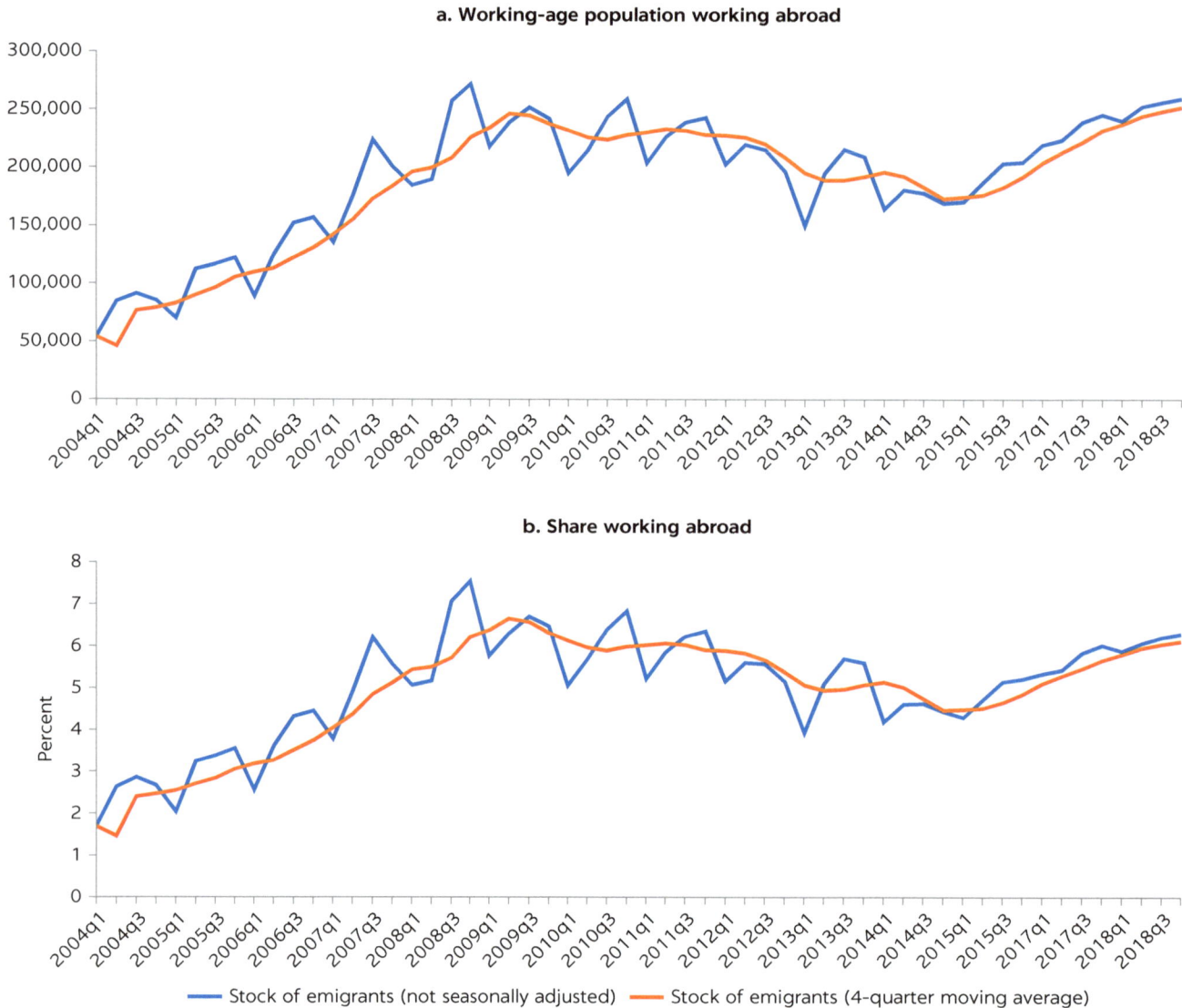

## a. Working-age population working abroad

## b. Share working abroad

— Stock of emigrants (not seasonally adjusted)　— Stock of emigrants (4-quarter moving average)

*Source:* Different rounds of the quarterly Kyrgyz Integrated Household Survey.

**TABLE 1.2 Correlations between emigration trends and economic development in the Russian Federation, 2004–18**

|  | LOG (PRICE OF RUSSIAN GAS IN RUBLES) | LOG (RUSSIAN REAL GDP IN RUBLES) | GROWTH RATE OF PRICE OF RUSSIAN GAS (IN RUBLES) | GROWTH RATE OF RUSSIAN REAL GDP (IN RUBLES) |
|---|---|---|---|---|
| Log (emigrants) | +0.80 | +0.82 |  |  |
| Growth rate of emigrants |  |  | +0.29 | +0.42 |

*Sources:* World Bank, based on IMF World Economic Outlook database, KIHS (2018), and national statistics.

extent of the migration phenomenon in the country. If one also considers permanent migrants based on statistics from the DESA database, an estimated 11 percent of the population born in the Kyrgyz Republic currently resides abroad. Recent data from the World Bank Listening to the Citizens of the Kyrgyz Republic survey for 2021 (L2CK) show that the stock of temporary labor migrants in 2021 remained significantly below pre-COVID-19 pandemic levels (~167,000, about 40 percent lower than in 2018).

Labor migration from the Kyrgyz Republic is often temporary, with relatively short durations of stay overseas. Beyond regular questions on workers with jobs overseas in the KIHS, the Listening to the Citizens of the Kyrgyz Republic survey includes a more detailed migration module with additional questions about household members currently abroad and returnees. According to this survey, the median time since departure of current migrants is quite low (7 months) and is similar to estimates from the KIHS (9 months) (figure 1.2, panel a). Close to two-thirds of current emigrants have stayed overseas for less than a year, while about 20 percent have stayed overseas for more than two years. The L2CK also asks respondents whether any member of their household had worked abroad during the 20 years prior to the survey. Based on that metric, there were about 650,000 returnees who had migrated in the previous 20 years and had returned at the time of the survey (10 percent of the total population and close to 20 percent of the working age population). Similar to estimates of time since departure of current migrants—which do not fully capture the whole length of migration as migrants have not yet returned— the average duration of stay abroad for returnees in 2021 was about one year, highlighting that a large part of migration in the Kyrgyz Republic is of a very short-term nature.

The short-term nature of migration episodes in the Kyrgyz Republic is largely planned by migrants. According to the KIHS, less than 20 percent of returnees reported unexpected negative supply shocks in their legal and employment status at destination as the main reason for returning. On the other hand, close to 20 percent returned in line with their premigration plans or because they had saved enough money, and close to 60 percent returned for family reasons or because they were homesick. Therefore, the motivations to return are largely unrelated to unexpected negative shocks from the destination country and are

**FIGURE 1.2**

**Distribution of length of stay abroad among migrant workers**

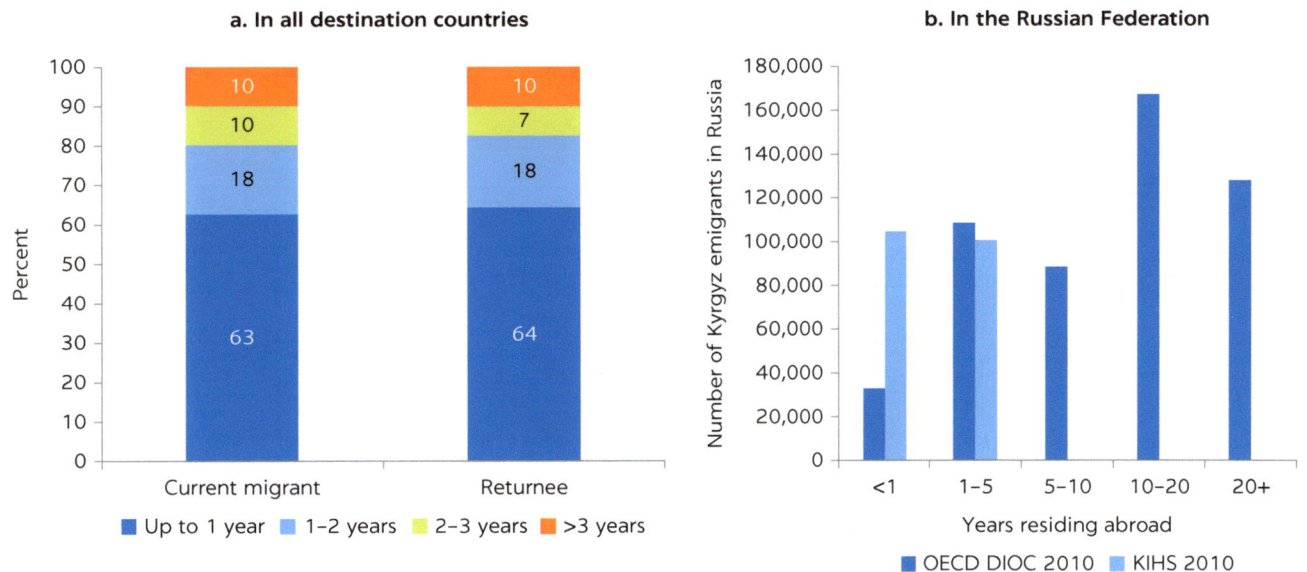

Sources: L2CK 2021, KIHS of 2010, OECD DIOC 2010 based on the Russian Federation census of 2010.

rooted on migrant decisions that are either predeparture or related to family issues.

However, administrative data in receiving countries (mostly the Russian Federation) provide a more nuanced picture, with a larger share of longer-term Kyrgyz migrants. Statistics based on questions on household members in the Kyrgyz Republic about their family members abroad might be biased and capture an incomplete picture of emigration from the country. For example, entire families might have left the country, or longer-term emigrants might stop being considered part of the household in the Kyrgyz Republic. Those migrant households would not be captured by the KIHS, as it only captures migrants who have remaining family members in the Kyrgyz Republic. According to the 2010 National Census of the Russian Federation, there were 528,000 Kyrgyz migrants living in the Russian Federation, while the Kyrgyz Integrated Household Survey (KIHS) only captured 205,000, which is less than 40 percent. Furthermore, while the KIHS shows short-term migrants (with migration durations of less than five years), the Russian Federation census estimates that close to 400,000 Kyrgyz lived in the Russian Federation for more than five years—so the majority of Kyrgyz migrants stay in the country for a long time (figure 1.2, right panel). Longer-term migrants also have higher levels of education: 23 percent have tertiary degrees, compared to only 10 percent of migrants found in the KIHS.

Migration in the Kyrgyz Republic also exhibits an important degree of circularity. According to the L2CK (2021), more than half of returnees had migrated abroad and returned home more than once during the last 20 years. The fluidity and cyclicality of migration are also observed by the large share of returnees who intend to migrate in the following year. More than one in four working age returnees in 2021 had a plan to remigrate within a year, compared to only 8 percent of nonmigrant adults (figure 1.3). These patterns are similar across age

FIGURE 1.3
**Circularity of migration from the Kyrgyz Republic**

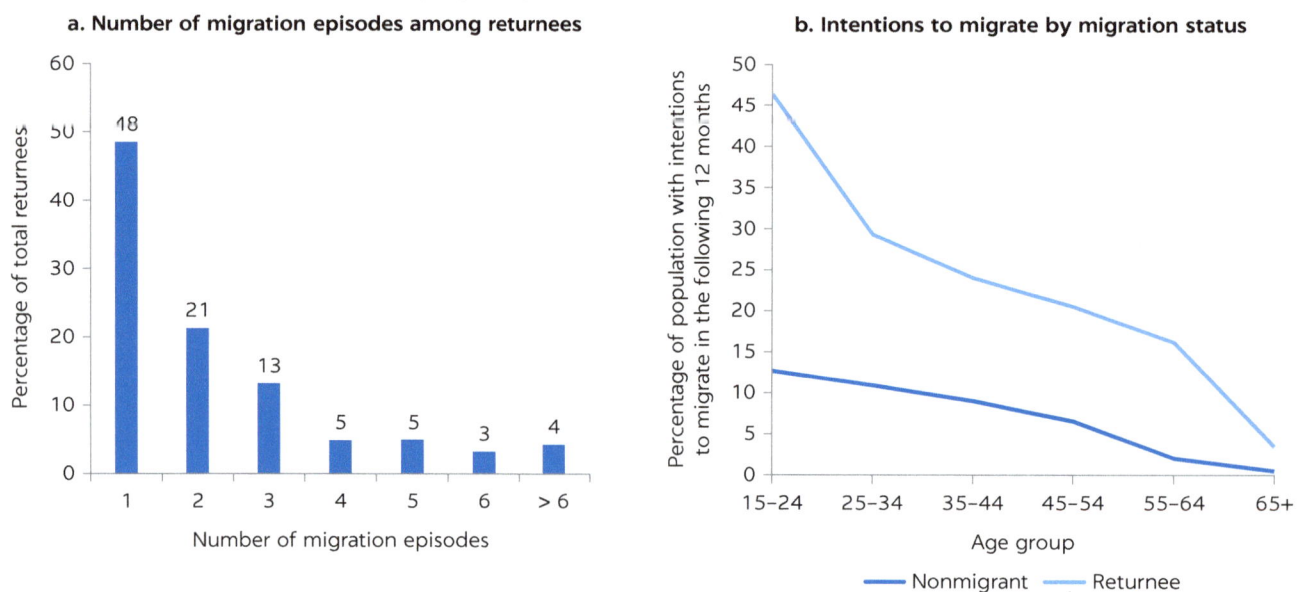

*Source:* L2CK 2021.
*Note:* "Intentions to migrate" is the share of the population in each group (returnees and nonmigrants) that responded intending to migrate in the next 12 months.

groups, although elder citizens are, as expected, less likely to have migration plans compared to younger cohorts. All these features of migration patterns in the Kyrgyz Republic make the distinction between emigrants and returnees less clear.

## DRIVERS OF LABOR MIGRATION FROM THE KYRGYZ REPUBLIC

Emigration in the Kyrgyz Republic is mainly driven by a lack of economic opportunities and the search for higher earnings. Past studies based on household surveys conclude that the vast majority of migrants leave the country because of economic deprivation, either to obtain higher earnings or due to limited domestic employment opportunities (Dubashov, Kruse, and Ismailakhunova 2017; World Bank 2015). The Kyrgyz Republic is currently experiencing a youth bulge resulting in a large number of new entries into the labor market every year: between 2004 and 2018, the working age population increased at an annual average of approximately 62,000 people, according to the Listening to the Citizens of the Kyrgyz Republic Survey. On the other hand, net employment creation only averaged 30,000 jobs per year during the same period, with more Kyrgyz, in particular youth, being unable to find employment. Beyond job availability, the quality of employment has remained low, with high degrees of informality, seasonality, and lack of tenure (World Bank 2015). Despite recent strong growth rates in wages in the country, there is still a large wage gap compared to main migrant-destination countries such as the Russian Federation.

At the regional level, this economic-based motivation for migration has resulted in poorer regions having higher emigration rates (World Bank 2015). According to the 2018 KIHS, the overall emigration rate in the Kyrgyz Republic (the number of emigrants over the total nonmigrant population) stood at 6 percent among the working-age population (figure 1.1, left panel). However, emigration rates were significantly higher in more rural and less developed areas of the western regions of Batken (14 percent), Osh (12 percent), and Jalal-Abad (8 percent). In contrast, temporary migration of workers located in the capital city of Bishkek is quite low (figure 1.4, right panel).

Beyond economic drivers, other factors shape migration flows. For example, the quality of public services in both origin and destination countries also constitute push and pull factors for migration. Evidence from other contexts shows that more developed education and health care systems and overall social safety nets in receiving countries attract migration flows (Geis, Uebelmesser, and Werding 2013; Pedersen, Pytlikova, and Smith 2008). Similarly, a lower quality and availability of public services increase the intentions to emigrate in sending countries (Dustmann and Okatenko 2014). More broadly, local amenities affect migration flows. Climate change and environmental degradation, which reduce livability of a place, can thus lead to more emigration (Afifi and Turner 2008). Weak governance is another factor found in cross-country analyses that incentivizes emigration, especially among higher skilled workers, as it hinders meritocracy and reduces the return to education (Auer, Römer, and Tjaden 2020; Cooray and Schneider 2016; Dimant, Krieger, and Meierrieks 2013).

In the Kyrgyz Republic, the processes of political and economic integration in the Eurasian Economic Union (EaEU) has also facilitated the mobility of

**FIGURE 1.4**

**Emigration, return rates, and correlation with poverty rates, by region**

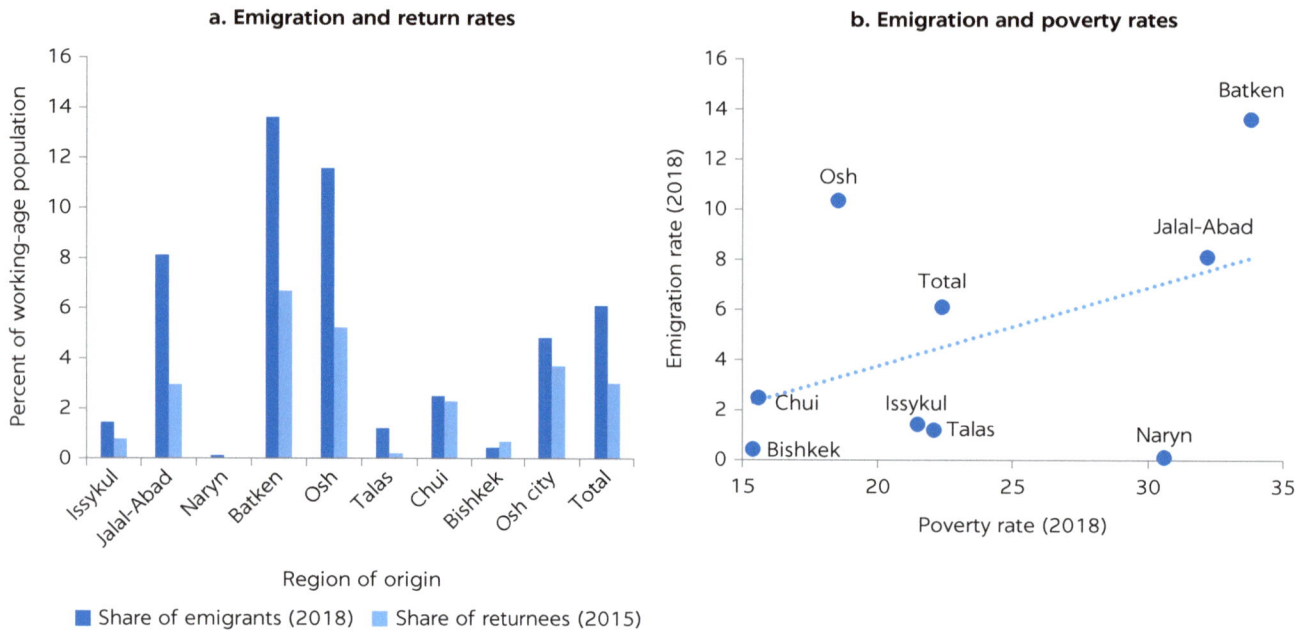

a. Emigration and return rates

b. Emigration and poverty rates

■ Share of emigrants (2018)  ■ Share of returnees (2015)

*Sources:* KIHS (2018) and KIHS migration module (2015).

Kyrgyz workers to other member countries, in particular the Russian Federation and Kazakhstan. The impact of the EaEU accession, which took place in 2015, on migration flows has not been rigorously studied, given data limitations. Looking at net international migration flows (inflows minus outflows), the negative balance (more people leaving than entering the country) has been reduced over the last years, not just in the Kyrgyz Republic but also in other neighboring countries, such as Uzbekistan and Tajikistan. However, contrary to the situation in the other two countries that have not joined the EaEU, the reduction in net outflows has been halted in the Kyrgyz Republic since 2016 (figure 1.5). Net outflows in the country, which were following a similar trend to those in Uzbekistan until the EaEU accession, have started to widen, which could suggest larger outflows given the reduction in legal mobility restrictions.

Networks also play a central role in supporting the migration process, from providing information, to providing financial aid and connecting to economic opportunities in destination countries. Social networks of relatives and friends are fundamental in facilitating migration. For example, the presence of a relative abroad is strongly correlated with a worker's decision to emigrate (World Bank 2015). According to results from the KIHS of 2015, close to four in five prospective migrants obtain the necessary information about the migration process through their network of relatives and friends, in particular those living abroad. Similarly, two-thirds of Kyrgyz migrants choose their country of destination based on the presence of a relative or friend. Once in the destination country, social networks also provide assistance in searching for a job. Previous evidence shows that the use of job referrals and networks by new immigrants make them more likely to find employment in the same occupations as older waves of migrants. Beaman (2012) studied the emergence of immigrant enclaves and networks in the labor market of destination countries

FIGURE 1.5

**Trends in net migration in Central Asian countries, 2012–20**

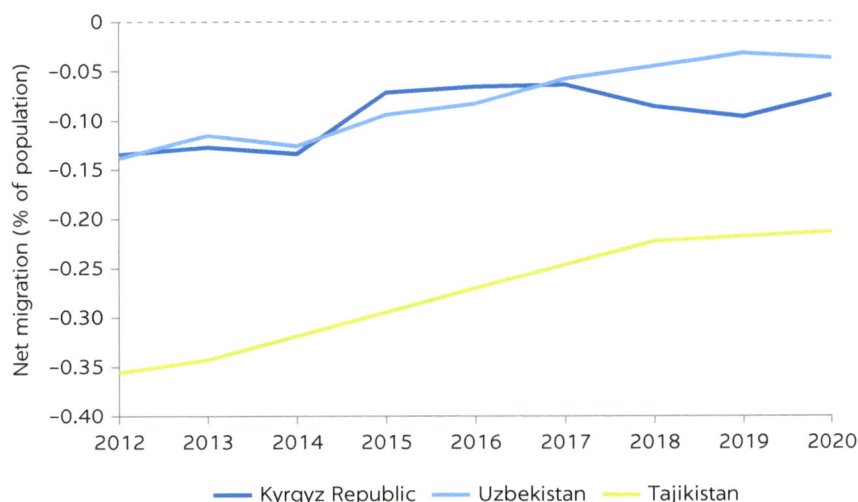

*Sources:* National Statistical Committee of the Kyrgyz Republic, State Committee of the Republic of Uzbekistan on Statistics, and Tajikistan Agency on Statistics.
*Note:* Net migration is defined as the difference between the number of immigrants and the number of emigrants for a given country in a given year, expressed as a percentage of the total population in the country.

and provides evidence that those networks in the different localities of residence influenced the occupational choices of different generations of immigrants. Similarly, Patel and Vella (2013) find that immigrants from specific countries cluster in particular occupations across different regions in the United States. This fact is not due to immigrants' skills or other characteristics but rather to the referral from previous cohorts of immigrants. Furthermore, those who work in occupations with a larger share of countrymen receive higher wages.

## PROFILE OF LABOR MIGRANTS

Temporary migration is concentrated among young males, while females represent a larger share of longer-term migrants. Data from the Kyrgyz Integrated Household Survey shows that temporary migration is a male-dominated phenomenon in the Kyrgyz Republic, with 78 percent of international emigrants and 76 percent of returnees being men (figure 1.6). However, as previously mentioned, the survey captures labor migration of a shorter or temporary nature. Broader statistics from the UN-DESA migration database exhibit a rather gender-balanced composition of migration (48 percent males), which contrasts with neighboring countries like Tajikistan and Uzbekistan, where migration is more concentrated among men. The age structure of migrants from the Kyrgyz Republic also widely differs from the general population. Among the working-age nonmigrant population, slightly less than 50 percent are between 15 and 34 years old, compared to 74 percent of emigrants and 70 percent of returnees. It is particularly striking that two in five current migrants are 15 to 24 years old, often leaving school to migrate and find employment abroad. As a result, the average age of nonmigrants (37 years old) is clearly higher than that of emigrants (29.5) and returnees (31).

FIGURE 1.6
**Demographic characteristics, by migrant status**

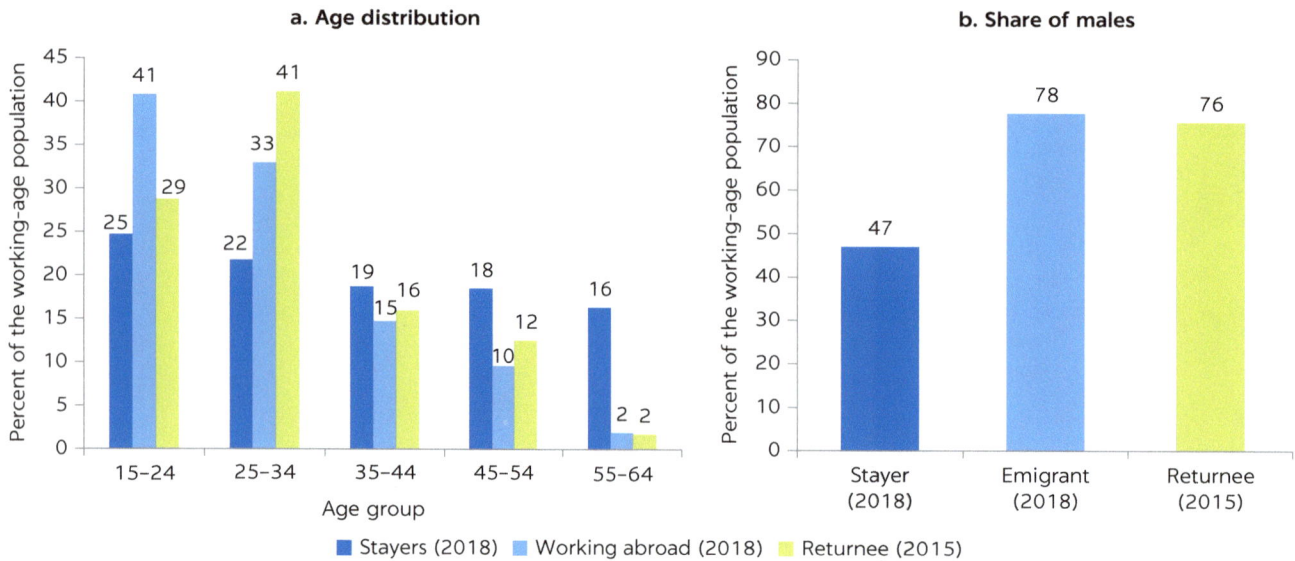

a. Age distribution

b. Share of males

Stayers (2018)   Working abroad (2018)   Returnee (2015)

*Sources:* KIHS (2018) and KIHS migration module (2015).

Kyrgyz migrants are overrepresented among the middle education levels compared to the general population in the Kyrgyz Republic. About 63 percent of Kyrgyz adult migrants (ages 15–64 years old) had completed secondary education in 2018, compared to 51 percent of Kyrgyz who stayed in the country (figure 1.7, left panel). On the other hand, migrants are underrepresented among low-skilled working-age adults with primary education or less (5 percent compared to 9 percent of nonmigrants) as well as high-skilled workers with tertiary education (11 percent compared to 17 percent of nonmigrants). As a result, the prevalence of emigration across education levels is higher for adults with secondary education (7 percent) and lowest for high- and low-skilled workers (4 percent). While the Kyrgyz Integrated Household Survey provides information on the education levels of short-term migrants, information from the Russian Federation's census shows that longer-term migrants are more likely to have higher education levels (figure 1.7, right panel). The educational profile of migrants can be linked to differences in economic returns to education as well as to financial constraints. Between 2004 and 2018, the average return to migration—defined as the wage differential between the host and home country–for a tertiary-educated Kyrgyz was 58 percent, significantly lower than those with secondary education completed (78 percent) or with lower education levels (87 percent).[2] The lower emigration rate among those with fewer years of schooling, in spite of having the largest returns to migration, might be associated with credit constraints that limit the capacity to finance the upfront costs of migration for poorer households. Indeed, about half of returnees in the KIHS of 2015 reported financing migration costs with their savings or asset sales, and almost another half through financial support of relatives. On the other hand, access to formal financial instruments is almost nonexistent, hindering the opportunity of poorer households to borrow for financing the cost of migration.

**FIGURE 1.7**

**Selection patterns in emigration**

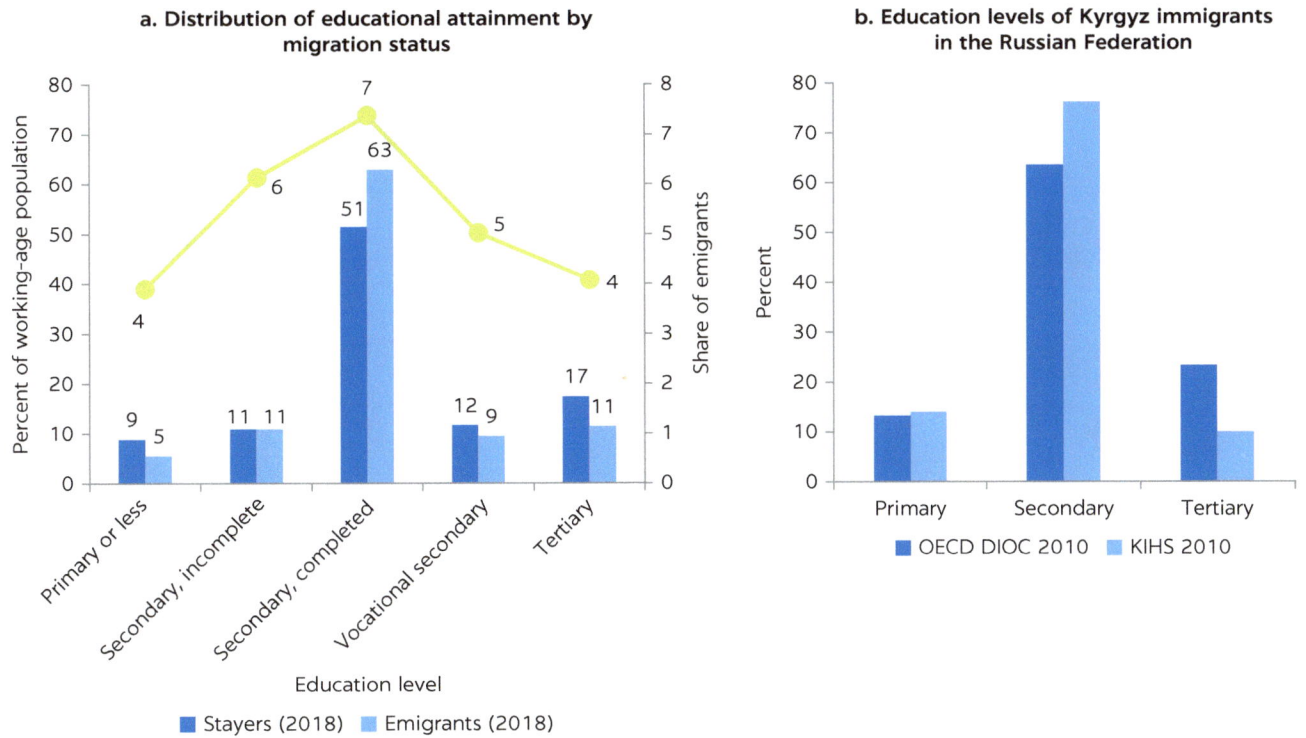

*Sources:* KIHS rounds of 2018 and 2010 and OECD DIOC based on the 2010 National Census of the Russian Federation.

While education levels are not systematically higher for Kyrgyz migrants, this population group tends to be positively self-selected in terms of skills. Many studies use education levels as a proxy for skill levels, given that very few surveys, in particular in developing countries, collect actual information on workers' skills.[3] In 2013, GIZ and the World Bank developed the Jobs Skills and Migration Survey, the first of its sort in the Kyrgyz Republic. Based on it, Ajwad et al. (2014) show that adults with intentions to migrate as well as those who returned from abroad possess higher cognitive and noncognitive skills than adults with no intentions to migrate. The results also suggest that studies focusing exclusively on education may draw very different (and potentially biased) conclusions.

## LABOR MARKET OUTCOMES OF MIGRANTS

### Premigration

Workers who migrate overseas had poorer labor market outcomes in the Kyrgyz Republic prior to migrating, compared to nonmigrants. The KIHS ad hoc migration module of 2015 provides further information on the premigration labor market history of migrants. While two in three nonmigrant male adults are employed, only 38 percent of emigrants had a job before migrating overseas (figure 1.8, panel a). On the other hand, while 9 percent of male

FIGURE 1.8

**Migrants' employment status before and during migration compared to nonmigrants**

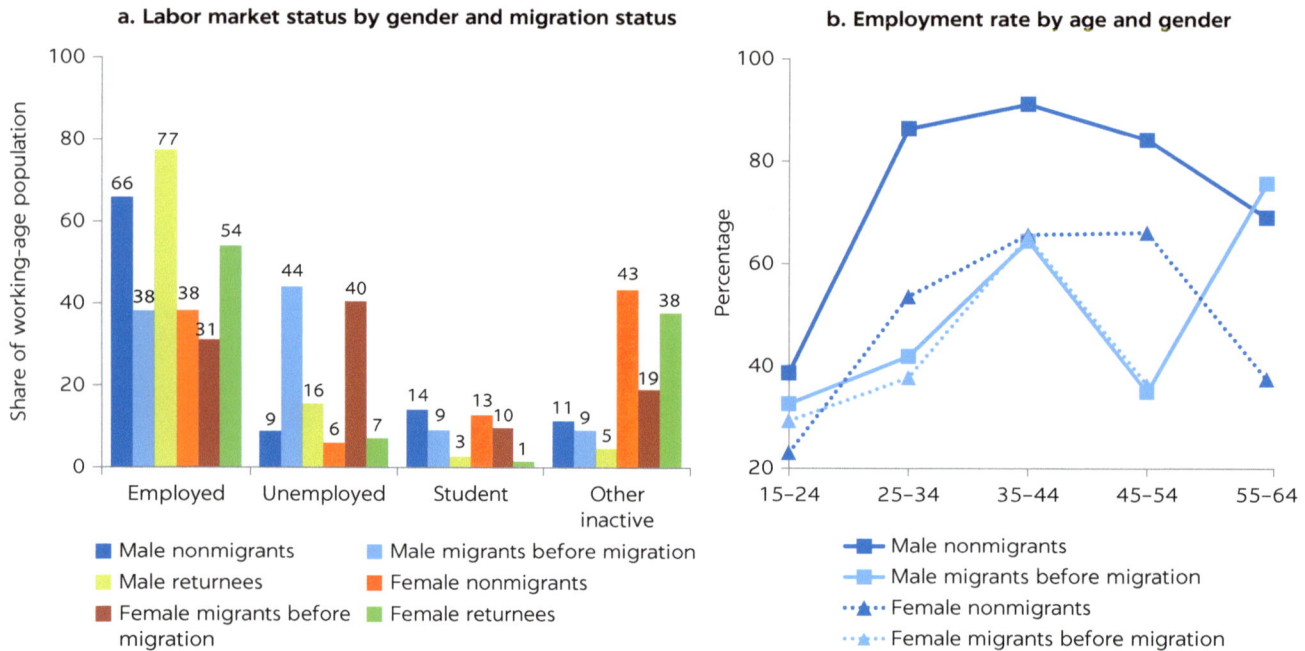

a. Labor market status by gender and migration status

b. Employment rate by age and gender

Male nonmigrants

Male migrants before migration

Male returnees

Female nonmigrants

Female migrants before migration

Female returnees

Male nonmigrants

Male migrants before migration

Female nonmigrants

Female migrants before migration

*Source:* KIHS migration module and regular employment survey (2015).

stayers were unemployed, this rate reached 44 percent among emigrants prior to migration. In turn, female migrants were more active in the labor market than female stayers by the time of migration (81 percent versus 57 percent of stayers), although this did not translate into higher employment but rather unemployment rates seven times higher. The negative self-selection of migrants' predeparture on labor market outcomes is particularly prevalent among the prime-age population (figure 1.8, panel b). The lower employment rate of migrants before migration persists after taking into consideration differences in education levels, gender, age, or oblast of birth. This indicates that migration is often triggered by "push factors," namely, unemployment and poor economic conditions in the home country. Migrants were also more likely to be studying by the time of migration (14 percent) compared to nonmigrants.

Migrants also have a different occupational profile than nonmigrants before migration. Before migration, not only are emigrants significantly less likely to be employed than nonmigrants, but they are also more likely to have jobs in lower-skilled occupations (figure 1.9). For example, about 12 percent of nonmigrant males and 30 percent of nonmigrant females worked in 2015 as managers, professionals, or technicians, occupations that require more complex tasks and skills, compared to only 1 percent of male and 15 percent of female prospective emigrants. On the other hand, more than half of male emigrants who were employed prior to migration were working as agriculture workers. Therefore, migrants self-select among those with poorer employment outcomes before migration—more unemployed or employed in lower-skill occupations, mostly in agriculture.

FIGURE 1.9

**Occupational status of emigrants before departure, during migration, and after return compared to nonmigrants**

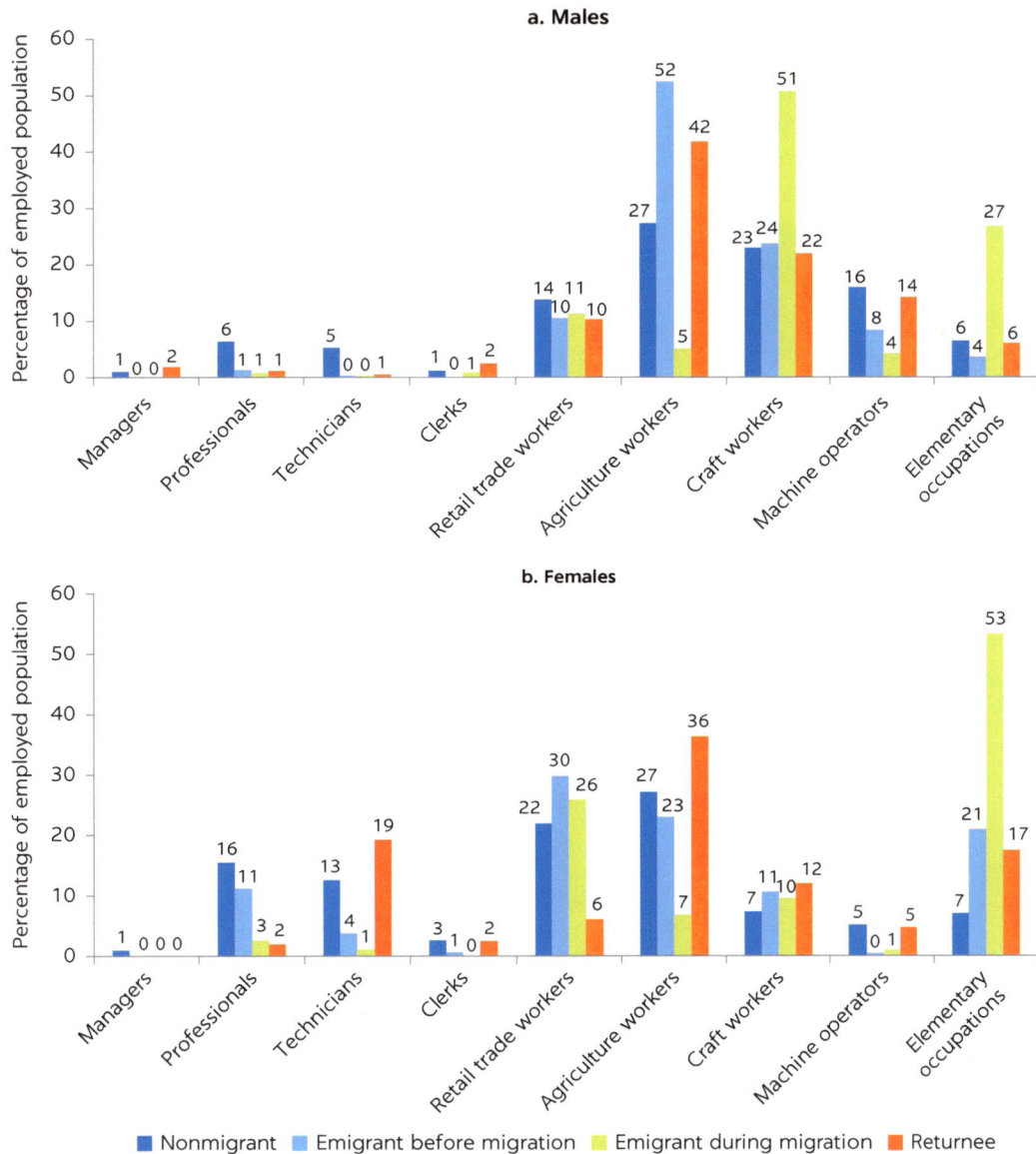

a. Males

b. Females

■ Nonmigrant ■ Emigrant before migration ■ Emigrant during migration ■ Returnee

*Source:* KIHS migration module and regular employment survey (2015).

## During migration

While abroad, migrants are employed in different sectors and occupations abroad compared to nonmigrants, with a general occupational downgrade. Compared to stayers, the vast majority of migrants from the Kyrgyz Republic are wage workers during their experience abroad: only 9 percent of men and 2 percent of women are self-employed overseas, as opposed to half of the employed population in the Kyrgyz Republic (figure 1.10, panel a). The sectoral gap is even larger, with 30 percent of male nonmigrants employed in the agricultural sector in 2015 compared to only 7 percent of migrants abroad (figure 1.10, panel b). These findings are similar among women. Agriculture represents 34 percent of employment for nonmigrants, 5 percent for current migrants, and 43 percent for returnees. While abroad, male international migrants are highly concentrated in construction and trade sectors and female migrants in the hospitality and trade sectors. In terms of occupation, about 82 percent of male emigrants and 63 percent of female emigrants worked in low-skilled occupations as craft workers and elementary occupations—mostly in construction and manufacturing in the case of male migrants—during their migration experience (figure 1.9). The majority of the remaining workers abroad had jobs in the retail trade and service sector.

**FIGURE 1.10**

**Type and sector of employment of migrants during and after migration compared to nonmigrants**

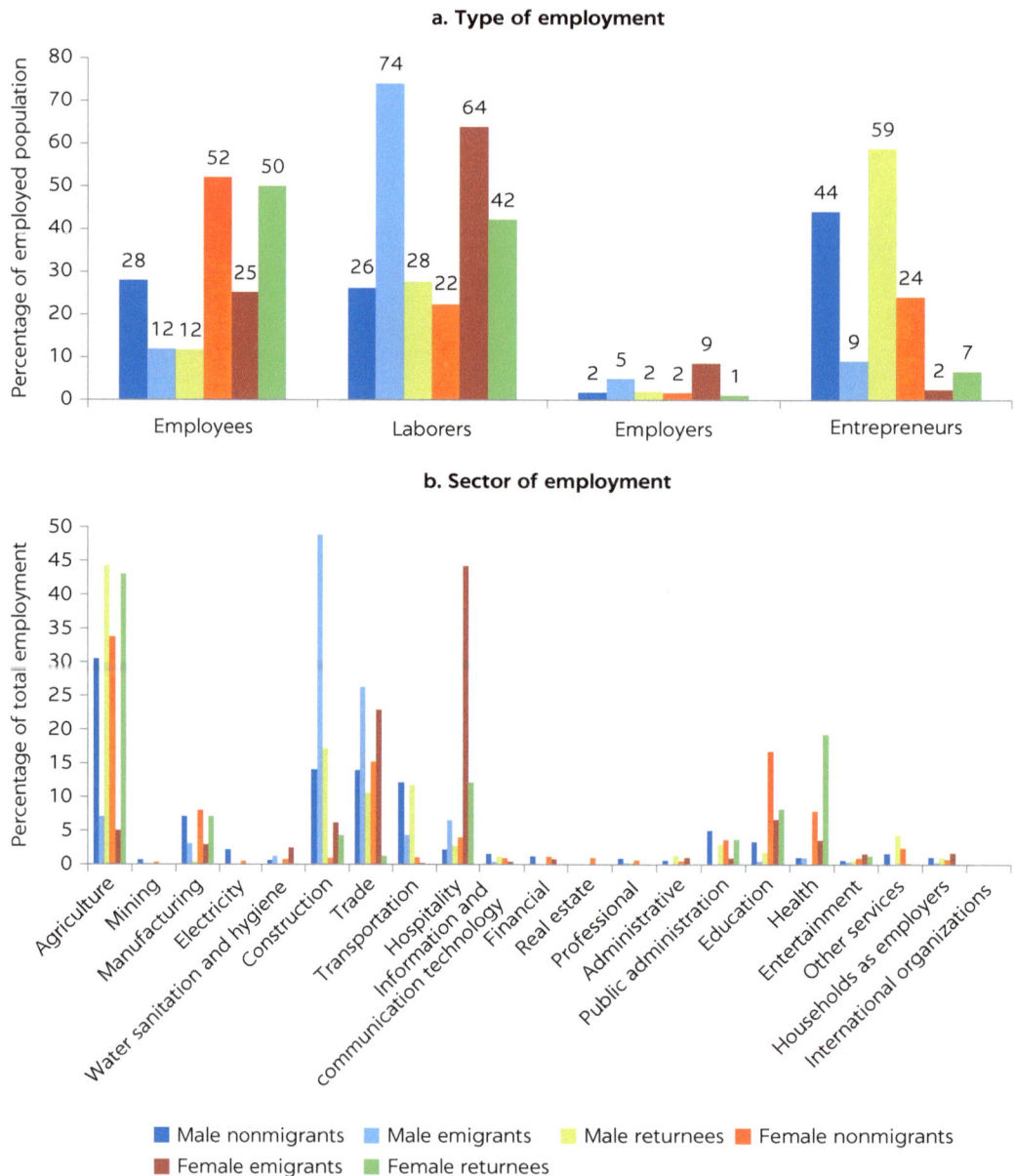

a. Type of employment

b. Sector of employment

Male nonmigrants    Male emigrants    Male returnees    Female nonmigrants
Female emigrants    Female returnees

*Source:* KIHS migration module and regular employment survey (2015).

Despite the occupational downgrade, Kyrgyz emigrants earn a high wage premium during migration, in particular those with lower education levels. Migrants obtain significantly larger wages abroad compared to nonmigrants across all education levels, even after taking into consideration differences in sociodemographic characteristics such as age, gender, education, or place of birth (figure 1.11 and figure 1.12, panel a). Since 2004, returns to migration have been higher for low-educated workers (87 percent), compared to mid-educated (78 percent) and highly educated Kyrgyz migrants (58 percent). The gaps are large despite the fact that migrants suffer some occupational downgrade while

FIGURE 1.11

**Wage premium earned by Kyrgyz migrants overseas compared to nonmigrants**

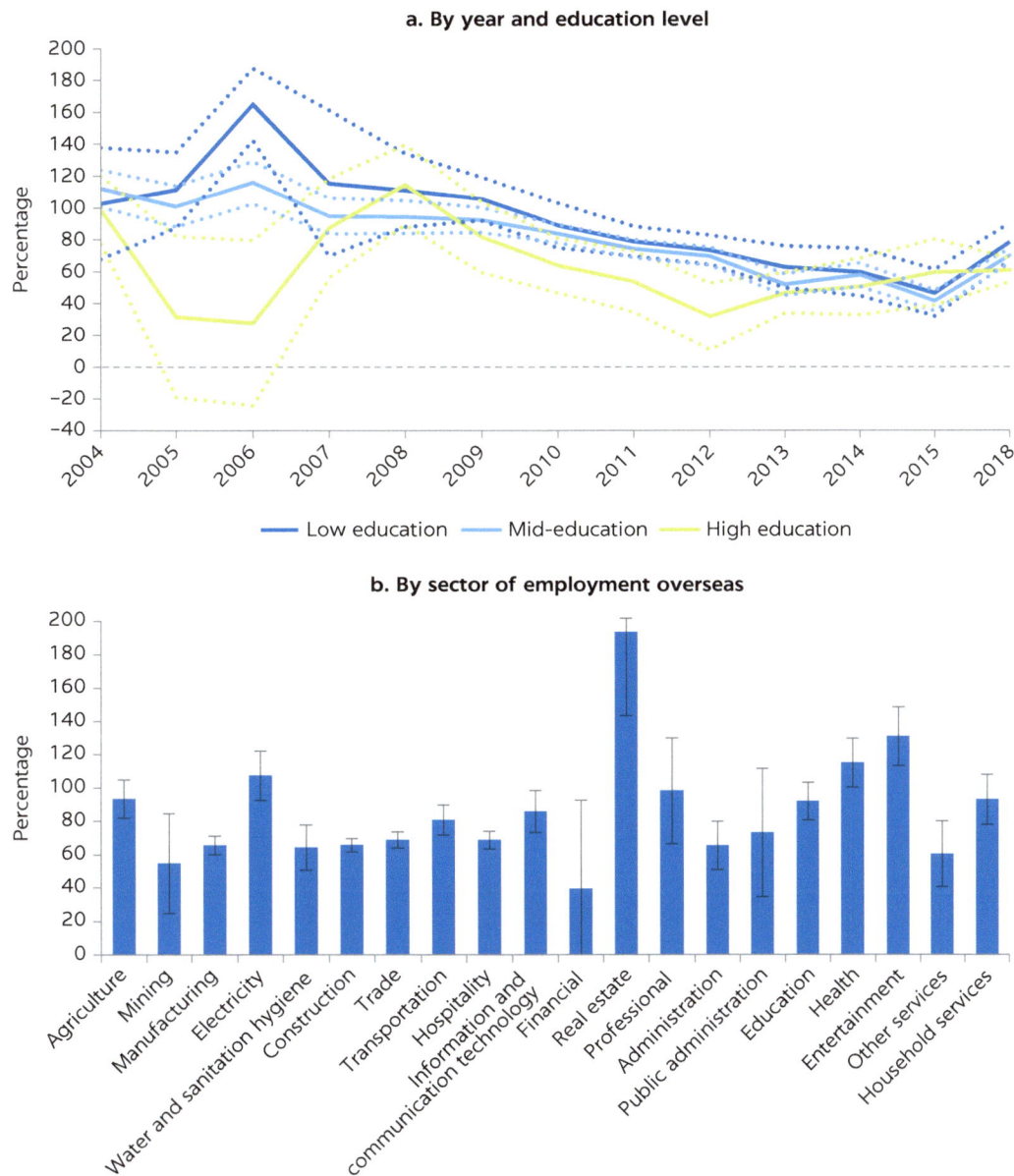

a. By year and education level

— Low education  — Mid-education  — High education

b. By sector of employment overseas

*Source:* Different rounds of the Kyrgyz Integrated Household Survey.
*Note:* Wage premium is the difference in percentage change in earnings between what Kyrgyz workers earn in the Kyrgyz Republic and what Kyrgyz migrants earn overseas, controlling for differences in gender, age, education, or region of origin. Dotted lines (bars) represent the standard error bands. Low education = those with less than upper secondary education; Mid-education = those with upper secondary education; and High education = those with tertiary education.

working abroad. Over time, a progressive decline in the returns to migration is observed, given the faster increase of wages in the Kyrgyz Republic (World Bank 2015). The reduction in the wage premium has been most pronounced among low-educated workers, but still in 2018 returns to migration were 25 percent higher for them compared to high-skilled workers. Migrants obtain a positive wage premium in all sectors of employment that is above 100 percent (doubling the wages in the Kyrgyz Republic) in the real estate, entertainment and recreation, and electricity sectors (figure 1.11, panel b).

## Postmigration

Despite the worse initial labor market outcomes, migrants are more likely to be employed upon return to the Kyrgyz Republic than nonmigrants. The positive gap is particularly large for migrant women (54 percent employment rates versus 38 percent for stayers), but it is also sizable for men (77 percent versus 66 percent) (figure 1.8, panel a). Larger employment rates for returnees are associated with higher participation in the labor force. In terms of unemployment, male returnees have slightly higher rates than male nonmigrants, while the opposite is true for female returnees. Differences in labor market outcomes between returnees and nonmigrants disappear in most cases when controlling for differences in sociodemographic profiles (such as age, gender, education, and place of birth). However, given that migrants were negatively selected in terms of labor market status at the time of migration, a better comparison for returnees is their premigration situation. Using this comparison, and even when controlling for changes in age and education, there is a significant employment premium associated with past migration for both genders, as migrants largely improve their labor market status upon return with higher employment rates and lower unemployment rates compared to their situation premigration.

Return migrants are often self-employed and work in occupations and sectors similar to their premigration experience rather than the jobs they had during migration. Three in five male migrants upon return are self-employed, which is

FIGURE 1.12

## Wages, by past migration status

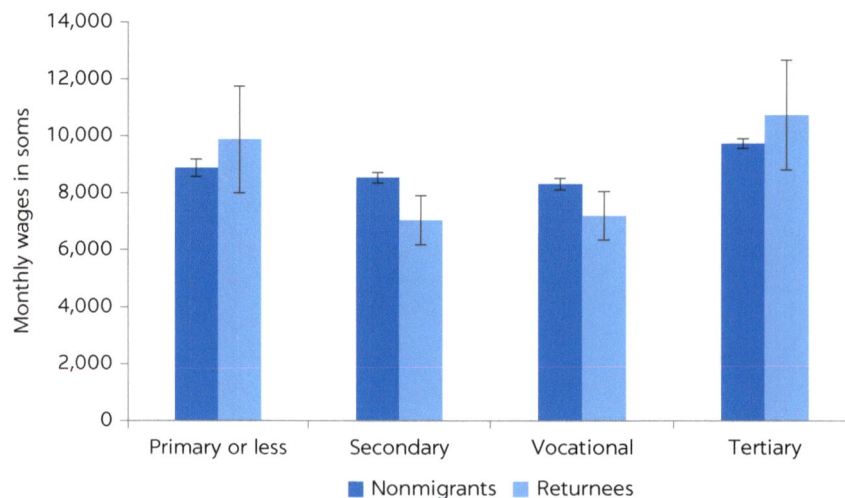

Source: KIHS migration module and regular employment survey (2015).

larger than the share of nonmigrants engaged in self-employment—about 50 percent (figure 1.10, panel a). The higher likelihood of return migrants to be self-employed also holds when taking into consideration differences in sociodemographic characteristics (age, gender, education, region of birth), and it is in line with results found in different contexts (Wahba and Zenou 2012; Wahba 2015; Batista et al. 2017). In many instances, this result has been used as suggestive evidence of migration promoting entrepreneurship, and in some cases, a causal link between temporary migration and entrepreneurship has been established (Batista et al. 2017, Bossavie et al. 2021; Yang 2006, 2008; Khanna et al. 2022). However, self-employment might be either returnees' choice or the consequence of limited employment opportunities as employees (the "parking lot" hypothesis of entrepreneurship of Harris and Todaro 1970). In the Kyrgyz Republic, Brück, Mahé, and Naudé (2018) provide evidence that self-employment among return migrants is often a temporary occupational choice, used until a better employment opportunity emerges. Also, they find that those migrants who were self-employed before migration were less likely to be so upon return, so migration might not be a financial tool that credit-constrained entrepreneurial workers use to save money for their entrepreneurial endeavors. In terms of sectors and occupation of employment, while many migrants change sectors during the migration experience, they switch back to their old sectors upon return to the Kyrgyz Republic—for example, 44 percent of returnees work in agriculture (figure 1.10, panel b). In the Kyrgyz Republic, returnees' occupational profile also matches very closely their premigration experience rather than their occupations abroad, with a slightly lower share for male agricultural workers while higher for females. Female returnees are also significantly more likely to be technicians than before migration.

In terms of earnings, migrants obtain similar wages than nonmigrants upon return to the Kyrgyz Republic, and there are no clear returns to past migration as in other countries (figure 1.12).[4] Given the small sample size of returnees in the migration module of the 2015 Kyrgyz Integrated Household Survey when dividing them by education levels, the wage estimates are somewhat imprecise. If anything, returnees earn slightly lower wages in the mid-education level (which is the vast majority of the migrant population), and higher for the lowest and highest educated. After controlling for other personal characteristics like gender, age, or oblast of residence, returnees do not earn wages that are significantly different from those of nonmigrants. The combined analysis of the labor market shows that the returns to work experience abroad are more apparent in the extensive margin—larger employment rates—than in the intensive margin—wage levels.

## IMPACT OF MIGRATION AND REMITTANCES ON THE HOME ECONOMY AND MIGRANT HOUSEHOLDS

The impact of emigration on a sending country varies depending on numerous factors and the time frame of analysis. Some of the main factors shaping the overall impact of emigration include the demographic profile of the country, the educational profile of migrants, the duration of migration and likelihood of return, links with the diaspora, the likelihood of remitting, and the human capital and financial accumulation during the migration period.[5]

As in other fast-growing regions, migration has slightly alleviated population pressures in the Kyrgyz Republic. Given the demographic transition in the country—where death rates have fallen rapidly while birthrates have increased since the early 2000s—the population has continued to grow. In the last decade alone, the population has risen by 20 percent (figure 1.13). While the natural change in the population contributed to an even larger increase (21 percent), net migration outflows slightly curbed the overall population increase. However, the size of emigration (1 percent cumulatively during the decade) was rather minor compared the rapid increase of the population.[6] In other migrant-sending countries, migration accelerates population aging, but given the youth bulge in the country and the high rates of migrants' return, aging is less of a concern in the Kyrgyz Republic.

There is no evidence of significant brain drain at the macro level, although emigration of high-skilled workers in certain occupations might create challenges. The emigration of a segment of the high-skilled population can reduce the average level of human capital in a country in the short run. However, the characteristics of emigration in the Kyrgyz Republic, where emigrants tend to be selected from the mid-education levels (those with upper secondary school) and a majority return to the country after a relatively short period of time abroad, alleviate concerns about a potentially sizable "brain drain." Cross-country analyses show that the brain drain due to emigration tends to be very low in countries in Central Asia (Docquier, Lohest, and Marfouk 2007). However, while there is no large negative impact of emigration on the human capital in the country overall, the emigration of workers in key occupations can create challenges such as labor shortages. For example, Adovor et al. (2021) find rising trends in emigration of medical professionals in Central Asia during the period of analysis of 1990 to 2014.

FIGURE 1.13

**Contributions of migration to population changes in the Kyrgyz Republic, 2011–20**

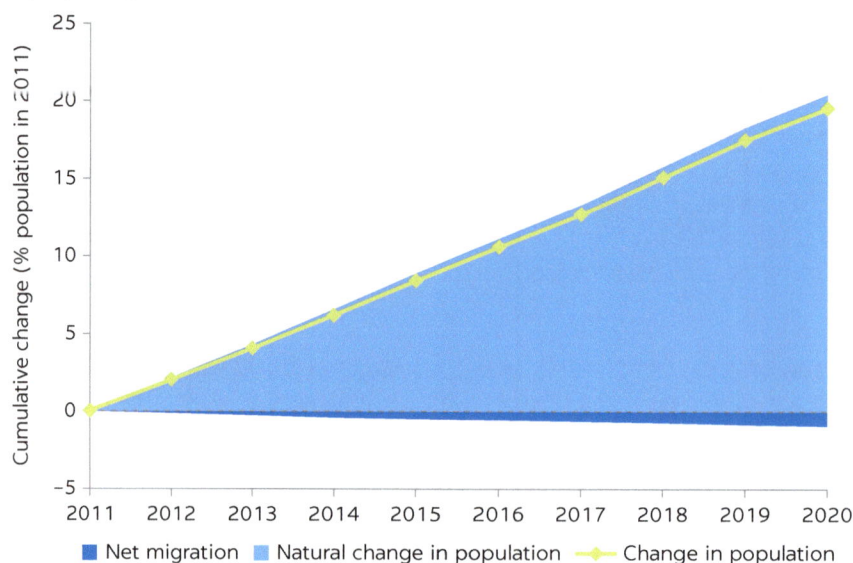

Source: National Statistical Committee of the Kyrgyz Republic.
Note: Net migration is defined as the difference between the number of immigrants to and the number of emigrants from the Krygyz Republic, in a given year.

Emigrants contribute to the Kyrgyz economy with a large inflow of remittances, the fourth-largest worldwide relative to the total size of the economy. Prior to COVID-19, the Kyrgyz Republic was one of the countries with the highest dependence on international remittances worldwide. Remittances represented 29.2 percent of GDP in 2019, making the Kyrgyz Republic the fourth-largest recipient country in the world, only after Tonga, Haiti, and South Sudan. At the macro level, remittances tend to be countercyclical, exerting a stabilizing effect on the economy and public finances (Chami, Hakura, and Montiel 2009; Frankel 2011). The countercyclical pattern also points at the key role of migration as a household economic diversification strategy to hedge against income risks like employment losses or underemployment of some of their members. In the Kyrgyz Republic, remittances have fueled economic growth, mostly by boosting household consumption, but they have been associated at the same time with some Dutch Disease–type symptoms such a loss in competitiveness through real exchange appreciation, an increase in the size of the nontradeable sector, and a fast growth of real wages (Dubashov, Kruse, and Ismailakhunova 2017).

In 2018, about one in five Kyrgyz households received remittances from abroad at least once throughout the year (table 1.3). Remittances are closely tied to the migration experience of household members. Migrant households can be defined as those who reported at least one household member whose location of work is abroad in any quarter from the KIHS (World Bank 2015). Among the 16 percent of Kyrgyz migrant households in 2018, 94 percent received remittances, compared to only 7 percent of nonmigrant households. Not only remittances reach a large share of the Kyrgyz population but, for those receiving them, they represented more than half (58 percent) of total income, more than labor earnings and other sources of income combined. In recent years, migrant households have become more reliant on remittance income, as in 2008 just over a third of total income in migrant households was from remittances (World Bank 2015). The higher dependence on remittances renders migrant households more vulnerable to economic shocks. For example, highly remittance-dependent migrant households in the Kyrgyz Republic can be pushed into debt when a migrant household member loses his or her job and stops sending remittances home (Thieme 2014).

TABLE 1.3 **Annual remittances and household income in the Kyrgyz Republic, 2018**

*In soms*

| MEASURE | NONMIGRANT HH | MIGRANT HH | TOTAL |
|---|---|---|---|
| HH income per capita | 51,195 | 79,667 | 55,679 |
| *Of which* | | | |
| Nonremittance income | 50,311 | 32,542 | 47,513 |
| Remittances | 884 | 47,125 | 8,166 |
| Remittances (% total income) | 2% | 55% | 10% |
| % HH receiving remittances | 7% | 94% | 20% |
| *Among HH receiving remittances* | | | |
| Remittances (% total income) | 29% | 58% | 50% |

*Source:* KIHS (2018).
*Note:* Average exchange rate in 2018: US$1 = 68.84 soms. HH = household.

Remittances are a powerful tool to increase household income in the country. Migrant households have, in the first place, lower income levels than nonmigrant families. The average annual per capita preremittance income of migrant households stood in 2018 at 32,542 soms (US$473), which is 35 percent lower than nonmigrant households. Taking remittances into consideration, the income per capita of migrant households increased to close to 80,000 soms (US$1,157), 55 percent higher than nonmigrant households. The higher income provided by remittances has been associated with better education outcomes (Amuedo-Dorantes and Pozo 2010) and health (Hildebrandt and McKenzie 2005). In the Kyrgyz Republic, remittances are mostly channeled to food purchases and housing improvements (Dubashov, Kruse, and Ismailakhunova 2017). On the other hand, migrant households spend a low share of remittances in investment and education. As a result, Akmoldoev and Budaichieva (2012) observe that migrant households do not spend more on education than nonmigrant households. In terms of educational outcomes, Kroeger and Anderson (2014) find that remittances do not improve the human capital of children left behind. In particular, dropout rates of teenagers aged 14–18 and malnourishment of girls in families that receive remittances are actually higher than for those in families with no remittances.

In terms of poverty rates, the literature has consistently found a positive impact of remittances on poverty reduction (Adams and Page 2005). At the national level, the poverty rate in the Kyrgyz Republic based on the national poverty line stood at 22.4 percent of households in 2018 (figure 1.14). However, in the absence of remittance income, another 8.2 percent of households would fall below the poverty line, increasing the share of poor families up to 30.6 percent. Remittances barely change the share of poor households among nonmigrant families—from 26.8 percent to 25.4 percent—given their low prevalence among this group. On the other hand, remittances help to significantly alleviate poverty among migrant households, reducing the share from 50.2 percent of families (excluding remittances) to only 6.7 percent.

**FIGURE 1.14**

**Poverty rate at the national poverty line in the Kyrgyz Republic, 2018**

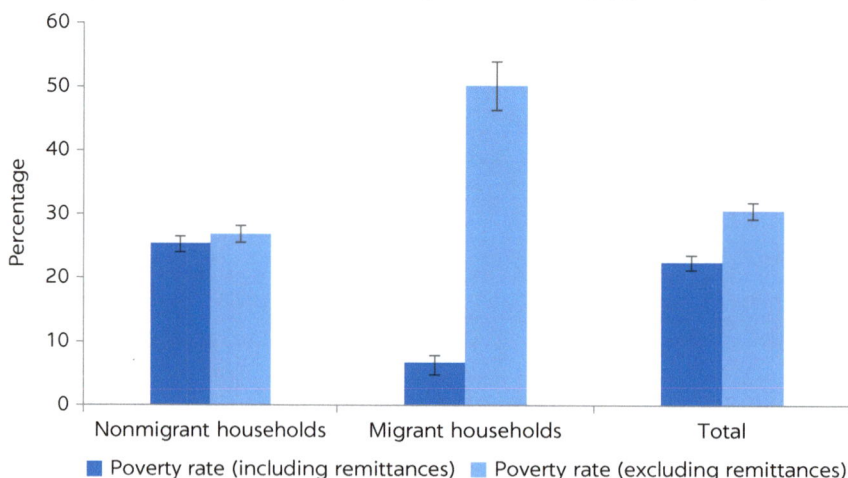

*Source:* KIHS (2018).

However, remittances may dampen labor supply among Kyrgyz households with international migrants. Larger disposable income as a result of remittances can have a negative impact on the incentives to work for nonmigrating family members.[7] This effect could thus reduce the labor supply and increase households' economic dependency on remittances. At the same time, by sending remittances back home, migrants can help family members left behind accumulate capital to start working as self-employed. The economic literature in other countries has mostly found negative effects of male migration overseas on women's labor supply at home, while the impact on men left in the country is less clear (Lokshin and Glinskaya 2009, for Nepal; Binzel and Assaad 2011, for Egypt; Mu and van de Walle 2011, for China; and Mendola and Carletto 2012, for Albania). According to the Kyrgyz Integrated Household Survey, only 63 percent of heads of households in the Kyrgyz Republic with migrants abroad worked in 2018, compared to 79 percent of head of households without international migrants. Controlling for differences in individual socioeconomic characteristics such as age, gender, education, and the region of residence, heads of migrant households are 11 percentage points less likely to be employed than in nonmigrant households. This result is similar to findings of past studies in the country (World Bank 2015). When looking at the employment rates of all nonmigrant members of the household, those who have a family member abroad are 5 percentage points less likely to have a job. Using a gender dimension, Karymshakov and Sulaimanova (2017) also find that women in migrant households are more likely to report having unpaid family work and increase the time for housework at the expense of less hours of work outside the home. Overall, there seems to be a negative correlation between migration and labor supply of family members in the Kyrgyz Republic, although a causal relationship has not been established.

## NOTES

1. The difference in the estimated stock of migrants from the Kyrgyz Republic between the two sources is primarily driven by the fact that the KIHS only captures short-term temporary labor migration by individual households, while excluding migrants that left the country for a longer period of time or for purposes other than for work, and entire households that left the country (World Bank 2015; Dubashov, Kruse, and Ismailakhumova 2017). In contrast, the DESA database considers all migrants from the country that are overseas. Beishenaly et al. (2013), relying on experts' evidence, increase the estimates of the stock of Kyrgyz emigrants up to 1 million (box 1.1).
2. Based on data from the KIHS, and controlling for differences in age, gender, year, and region of residence.
3. Perhaps the most important survey on adult skills in OECD countries is the Programme for the International Assessment of Adult Competencies.
4. In Eastern Europe, results show substantive income premia for return migrants, ranging from 40 percent in Hungary (Co, Gang, and Yun 2000), 10 to 45 percent in a selected group of EU New Member States (Martin and Radu 2010), to almost 100 percent in Albania (Coulon and Piracha 2005).
5. For a recent review of the international literature on the topic beyond the Kyrgyz Republic, see Bossavie and Özden (2022).
6. While migration is a prevalent phenomenon in the country, it is mostly temporary, and the actual outflows of longer-term migrants that are reflected in the statistics on net migration flows are rather limited.
7. For example, the wealth effect can increase the reservation wage of household members.

## REFERENCES

Adams, R. H., and J. Page. 2005. "Do International Migration and Remittance Reduce Poverty in Developing Countries?" *World Development* 33 (10): 1645–69.

Adovor, E., M. Czaika, F. Docquier, and Y. Moullan. 2021. "Medical Brain Drain: How Many, Where and Why?" *Journal of Health Economics* 76 (March): 102409.

Afifi, T., and K. Warner. 2008. "The Impact of Environmental Degradation on Migration Flows across Countries." United Nations University Institute for Environment and Human Security (UNU-EHS) Working Paper, UNU-EHS, Bonn, Germany.

Ajwad, M. I., J. de Laat, S. Hut, J. Larrison, I. Abdulloev, R. Audy, Z. Nikoloski, and F. Torracchi. 2014. "The Skills Road: Skills for Employability in the Kyrgyz Republic." World Bank, Washington, DC.

Akmoldoev, K., and A. Budaicieva. 2012. "The Impact of Remittances on the Kyrgyzstan Economy." Presented at the International Conference on Eurasian Economies 2012, October 11–13, Almaty.

Amuedo-Dorantes, C., and S. Pozo. 2010. "Accounting for Remittance and Migration Effects on Children's Schooling," *World Development* 2010 38 (12): 1747–59.

Auer, D., F. Römer, and J. Tjaden. 2020. "Corruption and the Desire to Leave: Quasi-Experimental Evidence on Corruption as a Driver of Emigration Intentions." *IZA Journal of Development and Migration* 11 (1): 7.

Batista, C., T. McIndoe-Calder, and P. Vicente. 2017. "Return Migration, Self-Selection and Entrepreneurship." *Oxford Bulletin of Economics and Statistics* 79 (5): 797–821.

Beaman, L. A. 2012. "Social Networks and the Dynamics of Labor Market Outcomes: Evidence from Refugees Resettled in the U.S." *Review of Economic Studies* 79 (1): 128–61.

Beishenaly, N., H. Levant, L. Ormonbekova, and C. Shamsiev. 2013. "Labor Migration and Human Capital of Kyrgyzstan: Impact of the Customs Union." EDB Centre for Integration Studies, Eurasian Development Bank, St. Petersburg.

Binzel, C., and R. Assaad. 2011. "Egyptian Men Working Abroad: Labour Supply Responses by the Women Left Behind." *Labour Economics* 18 (S1): S98–S114.

Bossavie, L., and Ç. Özden. 2022. "Impacts of Temporary Migration on Development in Origin Countries." Policy Research Working Paper 9996, World Bank, Washington, DC.

Bossavie, L., J. S. Goerlach, C. Özden, and H. Wang. 2021. "Temporary Migration for Long-term Investment." Policy Research Working Paper 9740, World Bank, Washington, DC.

Brück, T., C. Mahé, and W. Naudé. 2018. "Return Migration and Self-Employment: Evidence from Kyrgyzstan." IZA Discussion Paper 11332, Institute for Labor Economics (IZA), Bonn, Germany.

Chami, R., D. Hakura, and P. Montiel. 2009. "Remittances: An Automatic Output Stabilizer?" IMF Working Paper 09/91, International Monetary Fund (IMF), Washington, DC.

Co, C., I. Gang, and M. Yun. 2000. "Returns to Returning." *Journal of Population Economics* 13 (1): 57–79.

Cooray, A., and F. Schneider. 2016. "Does Corruption Promote Emigration? An Empirical Examination." *Journal of Population Economics* 29: 293–310.

Coulon, A., and M. Piracha. 2005. "Self-Selection and the Performance of Return Migrants: The Source Country Perspective." *Journal of Population Economics* 18 (1): 779–807.

Dimant, E., T. Krieger, and D. Meierrieks. 2013. "The Effect of Corruption on Migration, 1985–2000." *Applied Economics Letters* 20 (13): 1270–74.

Docquier, F., O. Lohest, and A. Marfouk. 2007. "Brain Drain in Developing Countries." *World Bank Economic Review* 21 (2): 193–218.

Dubashov, B., A. Kruse, and S. Ismailakhunova. 2017. "Kyrgyz Republic: A Robust Recovery with Underlying Weaknesses: Economic Update with a Special Focus on Labor Migration (English)." Kyrgyz Republic Economic Update 6, World Bank, Washington, DC.

Dustmann, C., and A. Okatenko. 2014. "Out-migration, Wealth Constraints, and the Quality of Local Amenities." *Journal of Development Economics* 110 (September): 52–63.

Frankel, J. 2010. "Are Bilateral Remittances Countercyclical?" *Open Economies Review* 22 (1): 1–16.

Geis, W., S. Uebelmesser, and M. Werding. 2013. "How Do Migrants Choose Their Destination Country? An Analysis of Institutional Determinants." *Review of International Economics* 21 (5): 825–40.

Harris, J.R., and M. P. Todaro. 1970. "Migration, Unemployment and Development: A Two-Sector Analysis." *American Economic Review* 60 (1): 126–42.

Hildebrandt, N., and D. McKenzie. 2005. "The Effect of Migration on Child Health in Mexico." *Economía* 6 (1): 257–89.

Karymshakov, K., and B. Sulaimanova. 2017. "Migration Impact on Left-Behind Women's Labour Participation and Time-Use: Evidence from Kyrgyzstan." UNU-WIDER Working Paper Series 119, United Nations University World Institute for Development Economic Research, Helsinki.

Khanna, G., E. Murathanoglu, C. B. Theoharides, and D. Yang. 2022. Abundance from Abroad: Migrant Income and Long-Run Economic Development." NBER Working Paper 29862, National Bureau of Economic Research, Cambridge, MA.

Kroeger, A., and K. H. Anderson. 2014. "Remittances and the Human Capital of Children: New Evidence from Kyrgyzstan During Revolution and Financial Crisis, 2005–2009." *Journal of Comparative Economics* 42: 777–85.

Lokshin, M., and E. Glinskaya. 2009. "The Effect of Male Migration on Employment Patterns of Women in Nepal." *World Bank Economic Review* 23 (3): 481–507.

Martin, R., and D. Radu. 2012. "Return Migration: The Experience of Eastern Europe." *International Migration* 50 (6): 109–28.

Mendola, M., and G. Carletto. 2012. "Migration and Gender Differences in the Home Labour Market: Evidence from Albania." *Labour Economics* 19 (6): 870–80.

Mu, R., and D. van de Walle. 2011. "Left Behind to Farm? Women's Labor Re-Allocation in Rural China." *Labour Economics* 18 (S1): S83–S97.

Patel, K., and F. Vella. 2013. "Immigrant Networks and Their Implications for Occupational Choice and Wages." *Review of Economics and Statistics* 95 (4): 1249–77.

Pedersen, P. J., M. Pytlikova, and N. Smith. 2008. "Selection and Network Effects—Migration Flows into OECD Countries 1990–2000." *European Economic Review* 52 (7): 1160–86.

Thieme, S. 2014. "Coming Home? Patterns and Characteristics of Return Migration in Kyrgyzstan." *International Migration* 52 (5): 127–43.

Wahba, J. 2015. "Selection, Selection, Selection: The Impact of Return Migration." *Journal of Population Economics* 28: 535–63.

Wahba, J., and Y. Zenou. 2012. "Out of Sight, Out of Mind: Migration, Entrepreneurship and Social Capital." *Regional Science and Urban Economics* 42: 890–903.

World Bank. 2015. "Labor Migration and Welfare in the Kyrgyz Republic (2008-2013)." Report 99771-KG, Poverty Global Practice, Europe and Central Asia Region. World Bank, Washington, DC. https://openknowledge.worldbank.org/handle/10986/22960?locale -attribute=es.

World Bank. 2016. "Systematic Country Diagnostic for Eight Small Pacific Island Countries: Priorities for Ending Poverty and Boosting Shared Prosperity." World Bank, Washington, DC. https://openknowledge.worldbank.org/handle/10986/23952.

World Bank. 2018. "A Migrant's Journey for Better Opportunities: The Case of Pakistan." World Bank, Washington, DC. https://openknowledge.worldbank.org/handle/10986/30272.

Yang, D. 2006. "Why Do Migrants Return to Poor Countries? Evidence from Philippine Migrants' Responses to Exchange Rate Shocks." *Review of Economics and Statistics* 88 (4): 715–35.

Yang, D. 2008. "International Migration, Remittances and Household Investment: Evidence from Philippine Migrants' Exchange Rate Shocks." *Economic Journal, Royal Economic Society* 118 (528): 591–630.

# 2 Risks and Inefficiencies of Labor Migration Exposed by COVID-19

The COVID-19 pandemic has severely restricted labor mobility in the Kyrgyz Republic and in the main migrant destination countries such as the Russian Federation, affecting both the push and pull factors of migration. From the supply side, many countries restricted mobility to prevent contagion, including mobility to work for those occupations not deemed essential. In the Kyrgyz Republic, the government approved different restricting measures such as establishing checkpoints in each city, and temporarily closing cafes, shopping malls, and other leisure events that entailed large gatherings (Dzushupov et al. 2021). On March 25, a state of emergency was declared in the three major cities of Bishkek, Osh, and Jalal-Abad, and residents were only allowed to leave their houses for essential services such as going to grocery stores, pharmacies, and medical centers. The government also prohibited interregion mobility in areas under state of emergency and closed the country's borders to foreigners. While the state of emergency was terminated on May 10, 2020, quarantine measures remained in place in the biggest cities of the Kyrgyz Republic. Therefore, restrictions affecting the capacity to engage in labor activities were more acute in urban centers than rural areas, where the majority of Kyrgyz migrant households reside, affecting the balance of pull and push factors of migration.

The COVID-19 pandemic resulted in unprecedented restrictions on international mobility, with very scarce availability of transportation to prevent the spread of the virus, derailing many migrants' plans and leaving them at high risk in destination countries. In the Russian Federation, the main destination country of Kyrgyz emigrants, the government also approved different mobility restriction measures, such as closing restaurants, nonfood retail stores, and other nonessential services from March to the end of April, depending on the region (Denisenko and Mukomel 2020). In cities like Moscow, restaurants, bars and cafes were also closed except for takeaways, and on April 13, 2020, car rental services, taxi services, and construction were also suspended. This disruption in the main destination countries reduced the strength of the pull factors of migration. The Russian Federation closed its borders at the beginning of the pandemic, with transportation being almost nonexistent. These restrictions remained until September 21, 2020, when it resumed international flights on a reciprocal basis with Belarus, Kazakhstan, and the Kyrgyz Republic

(Russian Government 2020). Many migrants who lost their jobs abroad could not return home, being stranded in the foreign countries without social protection. This disruption in the main destination countries also reduced the strength of the pull factors of migration. On top of these supply-side restrictions imposed by governments in the Kyrgyz Republic and migrant-receiving countries, citizens had also limited their mobility and consumption in a context of higher uncertainty and lower income.

The remainder of this report analyzes recently available databases to understand migrants' vulnerabilities brought to light by the COVID-19 pandemic and corresponding policy actions through the temporary migration life cycle framework (see box 2.1 on data availability in the Kyrgyz Republic since the COVID-19 outbreak). In contexts where temporary migration is widespread, such as the Kyrgyz Republic, the migration life cycle can typically be divided into four phases (World Bank 2018; Ahmed and Bossavie 2021): premigration decision, predeparture, in-service (while migrants are abroad), and return (figure 2.1). The first stage is predecision, when a worker decides to migrate based on their

**BOX 2.1**

## The limited availability of up-to-date data to assess the impact of COVID-19 on labor migration in the Kyrgyz Republic

The only nationally representative survey that provides information on different outcomes after the COVID-19 pandemic outbreak for both Kyrgyz emigrants and returnees is Listening to the Citizens of Kyrgyz Republic (2021). The largest survey post-COVID-19 to date is the one run by the National Statistical Committee of the Kyrgyz Republic (National Statistical Committee 2020). This survey was implemented between October 15 and November 15 of 2020 and interviewed 4,954 households, representative of urban and rural areas in all regions of the Kyrgyz Republic. In terms of migration, the survey only includes questions on whether households had a family member who could not return from abroad, or if they lost their job overseas and had to return home. However, it does not provide information on the broader impact of COVID-19 on the labor market, or income and health outcomes of current Kyrgyz migrants abroad, nor does it shed light on the current situation of those who returned to the country. In 2021, the World Bank implemented the Listening to the Citizens of the Kyrgyz Republic survey, a nationally representative survey of 3,203 households (and more than 15,000 individuals), which covered questions on both current emigrants and returnees. The IOM and UNICEF conducted a rapid needs assessment of the challenges migrant workers and their families faced due to the COVID-19 outbreak (IOM and UNICEF 2020), although the reduced sample size (147 households) and sampling procedure limit the ability to confidently generalize the results for the broader Kyrgyz emigrant population.

In the Russian Federation, there have been several post-COVID-19 surveys targeted to migrants, including migrants from the Kyrgyz Republic, although they all have problems of representativeness. Perhaps the survey with the largest number of Kyrgyz migrants was run by Vershaver, Ivanova, and Rocheva (2020), who used advertising targeting on the social media platforms Vkontakte and Instagram to interview 2,074 migrants from April 23 to May 19, 2020, both across the Russian Federation and in Moscow specifically. Of those, 587 migrants were citizens of the Kyrgyz Republic. Denisenko and Mukomel (2020) surveyed 1,400 migrants in the Russian Federation as well as 1,300 potential migrants abroad both through social media and the telephone, although no specific results are disaggregated by country of origin. Finally, Ryazantsev and Khramova (2020) conducted a survey of more than 700 labor migrants from Central Asian countries in the Russian Federation in April 2020, of which about 10 percent were citizens of the Kyrgyz Republic.

**FIGURE 2.1**

**Migration life cycle stages and COVID-19 disruptions**

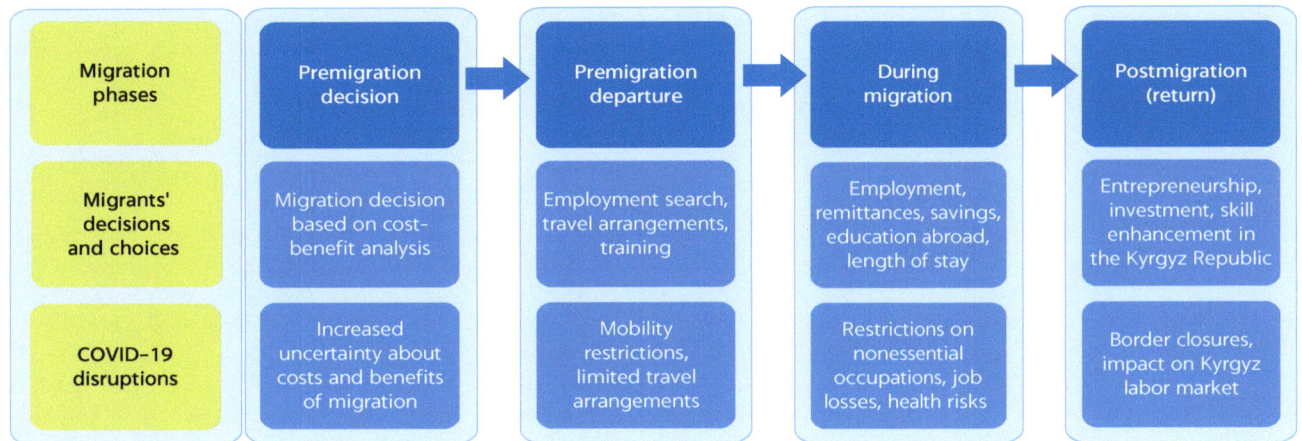

| Migration phases | Premigration decision | Premigration departure | During migration | Postmigration (return) |
| --- | --- | --- | --- | --- |
| Migrants' decisions and choices | Migration decision based on cost-benefit analysis | Employment search, travel arrangements, training | Employment, remittances, savings, education abroad, length of stay | Entrepreneurship, investment, skill enhancement in the Kyrgyz Republic |
| COVID-19 disruptions | Increased uncertainty about costs and benefits of migration | Mobility restrictions, limited travel arrangements | Restrictions on nonessential occupations, job losses, health risks | Border closures, impact on Kyrgyz labor market |

*Sources:* World Bank, adapted from World Bank (2018) and Ahmed and Bossavie (2022).

understanding of the costs and benefits of migrating. The second stage is predeparture, when after the worker has decided to pursue an overseas job, they can take up measures to improve their employability, finding and obtaining a job, and obtaining the necessary legal documents to migrate (clearances from national authorities, visas and passports, inter alia), and completing the logistical preparations for migration (for example, tickets, financing). The third stage is during migration, when the migrant is employed overseas. The final stage is after migration, when a migrant leaves the destination to return home and, in most cases, starts an economic activity in home labor markets. The decisions and outcomes of temporary migrants in each of these stages have suffered serious disruptions from the COVID-19 pandemic.

## PREDECISION AND PREDEPARTURE

Mobility disruptions, border closures, and limited travel options have affected the ability of many prospective migrants to move abroad and the costs and benefits associated with this decision. Prospective migrants make the decision to migrate analyzing the expected costs and benefits. The COVID-19 pandemic rapidly increased health concerns and mobility restrictions aiming at controlling the spread of the virus, severely limited the ability to work. While both health concerns and mobility restrictions were widespread across the globe, they have shown asymmetric effects across countries and regions, affecting the decision of prospective migrants by changing the relative costs and benefits of migrating to different countries. In theory, and other things being equal, a worker would prefer to migrate when the relative economic and health conditions are better in the destination country compared to their region of origin.

In terms of COVID-19 incidence, the Kyrgyz Republic has recorded a lower number of cases compared to the Russian Federation, the main migration-receiving country. The number of COVID-19 cases during the first wave of the pandemic in the Kyrgyz Republic was limited compared to

FIGURE 2.2
**COVID-19 cases and deaths per 1,000,000 inhabitants**

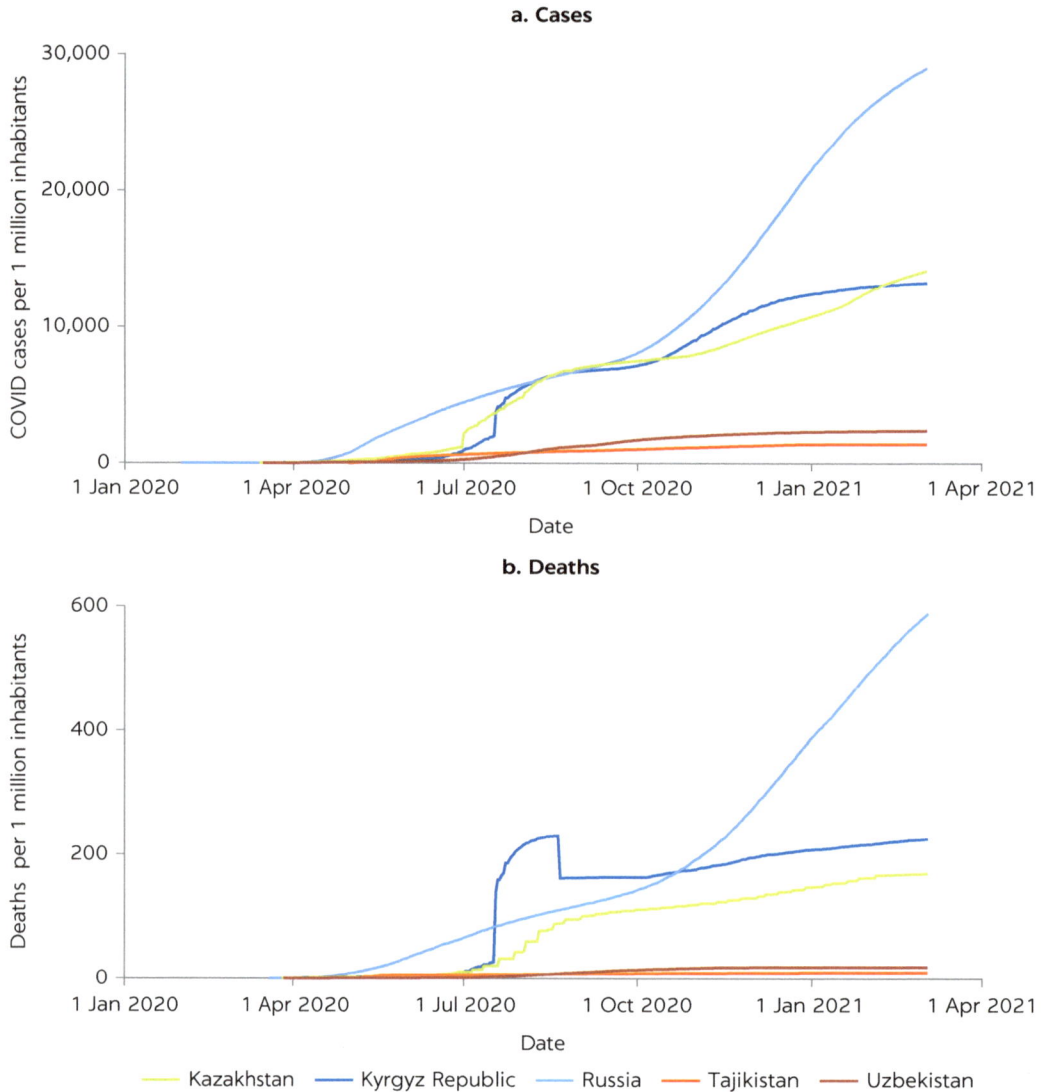

### a. Cases

### b. Deaths

Legend: Kazakhstan — Kyrgyz Republic — Russia — Tajikistan — Uzbekistan

Sources: Roser, Ritchie, Ortiz-Osina and Hasell (2020).

international standards but increased more rapidly during the summer and winter of 2020 (figure 2.2). At the beginning of March 2021, the Kyrgyz Republic reported more than 13,000 cases per one million inhabitants (1.3 percent of the total population). While still relatively low by international standards, the prevalence of the disease was significantly higher than neighboring countries of Central Asia such as Uzbekistan (2,400 per one million inhabitants) or Tajikistan (1,400 per one million inhabitants). On the other hand, COVID-19 cases have been more prevalent in the main destination country of Kyrgyz emigrants. The Russian Federation, with around 30,000 cases per 1 million, more than double the rate in the Kyrgyz Republic, while in Kazakhstan, the second-largest recipient country of Kyrgyz migrants, the incidence has been fairly similar. The statistics of deaths related to COVID-19 show similar cross-country patterns, with 600 deaths per million residents in the Russian Federation, three times more than in the Kyrgyz Republic and Kazakhstan.

Both the Kyrgyz Republic and the main host countries of Kyrgyz migrants have restricted mobility since the onset of the pandemic, limiting the opportunity for labor migration. According to Google mobility data, there was a drastic reduction in mobility to the place of work in the Kyrgyz Republic and main destination countries such as the Russian Federation and Kazakhstan. Both the Russian Federation and Kazakhstan had a maximum reduction in mobility of about 50 percent during April 2020 and, after a slight deterioration during the summer, slowly improved to about 20 percent in December 2020 (figure 2.3, panel a). As of March 2021, mobility to work still had not recovered prepandemic levels,

**FIGURE 2.3**

## Changes in mobility to work during the COVID-19 pandemic, 2020–21

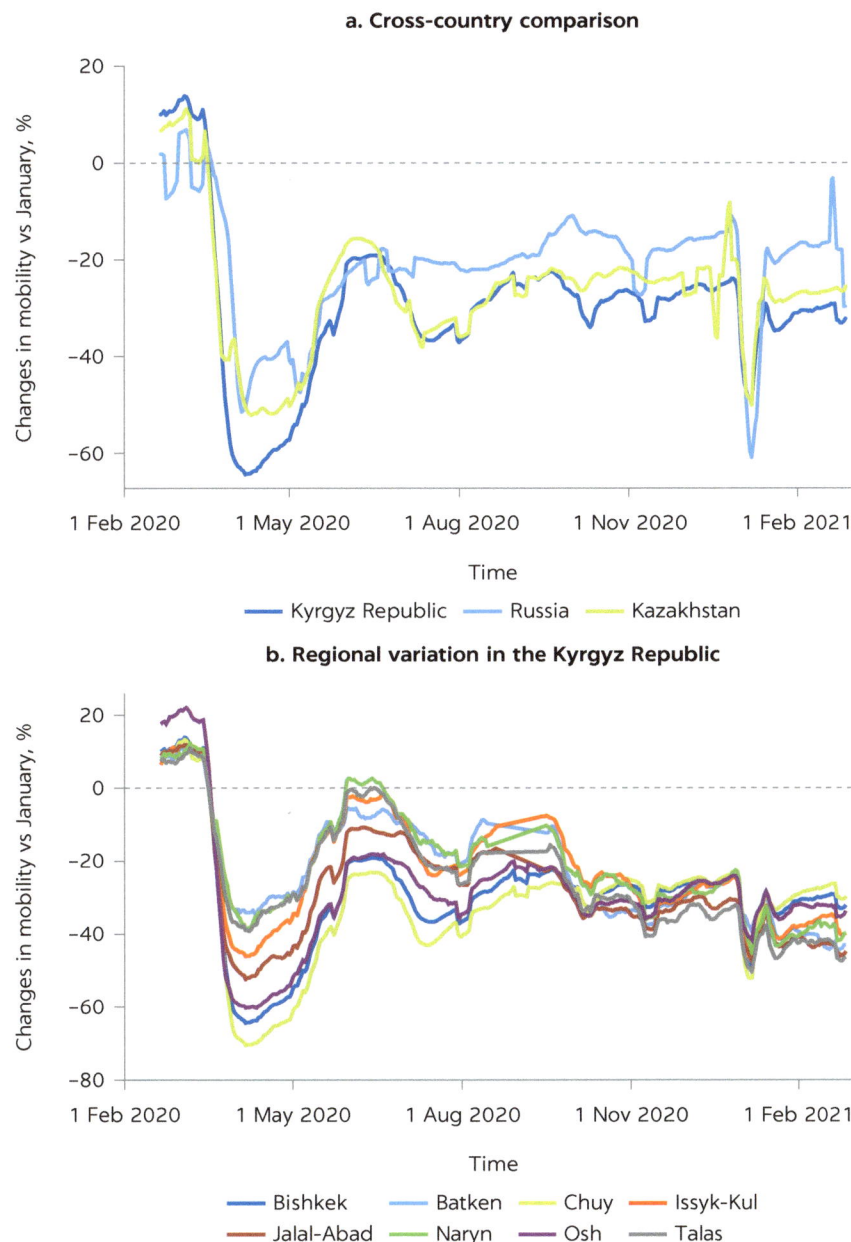

### a. Cross-country comparison

### b. Regional variation in the Kyrgyz Republic

*Sources:* Google LLC, "Google COVID-19 Community Mobility Reports," https://www .google.com/covid19/mobility.

showing a 30 percent reduction. In the Kyrgyz Republic, similar trends are observed, with commuting to work at the peak of the COVID-19 pandemic in early April 2020 dropping by 60 percent in the country as a whole. While mobility trends have been quite similar across these countries, the reduction has been more acute in the Kyrgyz Republic compared to the Russian Federation. However, rural regions in the Kyrgyz Republic where most migrant households reside—in particular in Batken, Jalal Abad, and Osh—showed a more limited reduction in mobility compared to urban centers such as Osh city of Bishkek (figure 2.3, panel b). These large variations across regions in the Kyrgyz Republic are the result of the asymmetric government policy that concentrated the state of emergency in the main urban centers. Overall, the higher mobility restrictions to work in urban centers, combined with the prohibition to enter these urban centers under a state of emergency, might have caused a reduction in internal migration. However, since autumn 2020, geographic mobility patterns seem to have shifted, with more rural regions having a progressive deterioration (larger than 40 percent reduction in March 2021) while remaining stable in Bishkek and Osh (around 30 percent).

The COVID-19 pandemic might have also exacerbated the imperfect information prospective migrants have about returns to migration. Recent evidence in different contexts shows migrants tend to have inaccurate information on the returns to migration. Some studies find that migrants underestimate potential earnings (McKenzie, Gibson, and Stillman 2013; Seshan and Zubrickas 2017), while others observe an overestimation of the economic returns abroad (Shrestha 2020). Migrants also have imperfect information on other migration costs such as the risks of work-related deaths at destination (Shrestha 2020) or the probability of obtaining legal status at destination (Bah and Batista 2020). Prospective migrants heavily rely on reduced informal networks. According to the ad hoc migration module of the 2015 Kyrgyz Integrated Household Survey, four in five return migrants relied on family and friends either abroad or in the Kyrgyz Republic to obtain information on where to migrate and how to find a job overseas. Overall, the consequences of imperfect information are estimated to be very large, increasing total costs for migrants by about 40 percent (Porcher 2020). The COVID-19 pandemic not only has lowered employment opportunities abroad but also has drastically increased the levels of uncertainty and volatility in the global economy, hindering the capacity of prospective migrants to acquire information and make informed decisions about the costs and benefits of migration. Uncertainties remain regarding migration and visa policies in destination countries, mobility restrictions, or on-the-job safety conditions, to name a few. Also, COVID-19 has proved to affect the sectoral composition of labor demand not only in the short term but also potentially in the longer term, with uncertainty about the strength of the future recovery of occupations with a traditionally high demand of migrants as tourism and hospitality, while other sectors have rapidly grown in the new context such as delivery services. Prolonged travel restrictions may induce additional technological change in certain sectors heavily relying on migrant labor, reducing future demand (Clemens, Lewis, and Postel 2018).

The COVID-19 pandemic led to a drastic drop in demand for migrant labor in the main destination countries, revealing the high exposure of migration flows to shocks at destination. In 2020, the Russian Federation granted work visas to 190,000 Kyrgyz citizens, less than half of the work authorizations issued in 2019 (454,000). Compared to the same quarter in 2019, the Russian Federation approved 78,000 fewer work visas in the second quarter of 2020, 108,000 fewer in the third quarter, and 72,000 fewer in the fourth quarter (figure 2.4). That is,

FIGURE 2.4

**Change in the number of visas authorized by the Russian Federation to Kyrgyz citizens, compared to the same quarter in the previous year, 2018–20**

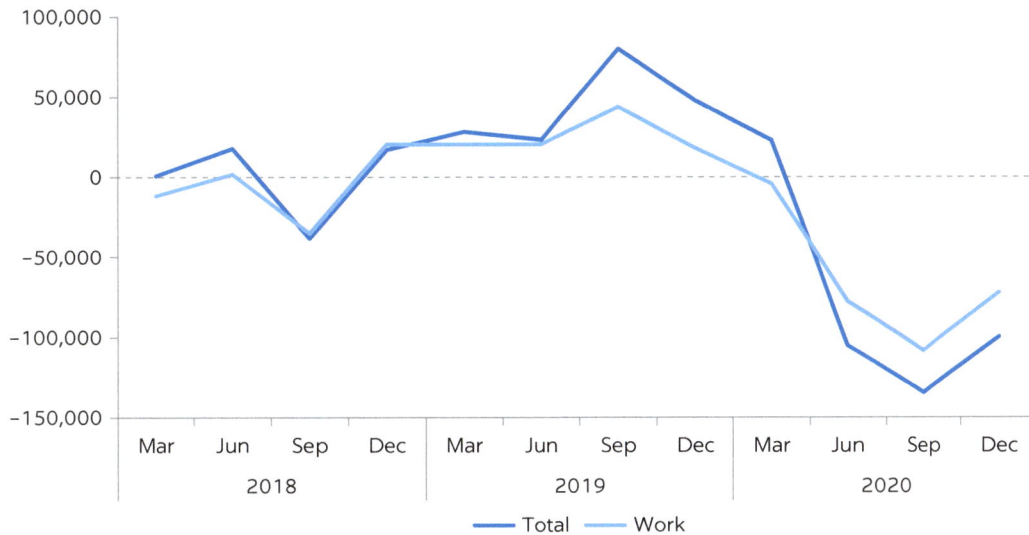

*Source:* The Russian Federation Federal State Statistics Service.

between March and December 2020, there were 258,000 fewer visas for Kyrgyz workers to legally work in the Russian Federation compared to the same period of 2019. These recent trends point at a drastic limitation of labor migration as a poverty alleviation tool in the Kyrgyz Republic, putting further pressures on the Kyrgyz labor market. While migration from the Kyrgyz Republic picked up again in 2021, statistics from the L2CK survey show that there were 167,000 temporary migrants abroad, about 40 percent fewer than the peak observed during the pandemic.

As a result, many potential migrants and their households had their migration plans disrupted due to COVID-19-related mobility restrictions. The survey on the impact of the COVID-19 pandemic run by the National Statistics Committee (2020) in October 2020 shows a drastic disruption in emigration plans. About 9 percent of Kyrgyz households had at least one member who cancelled their travel plans abroad. Given that there are about 1.57 million households in the country, this share means that close to 150,000 households had at least one member who could not travel abroad as planned. More precisely, the Listening to the Citizens of the Kyrgyz Republic survey of 2021 estimates that 174,000 individuals, which is about 2.6 percent of the population (and 5.5 percent of the working age population, were planning to migrate in the previous 12 months (between the summer of 2020 and 2021) but could not do so due to COVID-19. Taking into consideration that about 250,000 Kyrgyz emigrate every year for a short-term period—based on KIHS statistics—the number of disrupted migration plans was very large and temporary emigration came to a near complete halt. Furthermore, regions with higher numbers of migrants currently living abroad tend to have a larger share of households that could not migrate as planned, although the correlation is far from perfect. For example, Talas, a region with traditionally low to moderate emigration rates, had the second-largest share of households with disrupted migration plans (19 percent), only after Jalal-Abad.

Households with members that are forced to cancel their migration plans remain in a vulnerable situation in the Kyrgyz Republic, with limited employment opportunities and poorer health conditions. While individual-level labor market data are not available for 2020, the household survey implemented by the National Statistics Committee in October 2020 shows the sizable disruption of the COVID-19 pandemic on employment opportunities, with 19.7 percent of interviewed households reporting at least one member who lost their job between March and October. It is hard to estimate changes in employment rates based on this metric, as it only shows the flows from employment to unemployment (or out of the labor force) while there is no information on potential disruptions in the flows in the opposite direction. Furthermore, there is no straightforward translation of data at the household level to the individual level that is typically used in labor force surveys. If not all employed members of households reporting job losses lost their job post-COVID-19, then the drop in employment at the individual level would be lower than the 19.7 percent mentioned above. As highlighted by the literature on job vulnerability in the COVID-19 pandemic across countries, lower-income households in the Kyrgyz Republic suffered significantly larger employment losses.[1] Furthermore, the COVID-19 survey in the Kyrgyz Republic shows that households with a member unable to migrate were twice as likely to report employment losses during the pandemic compared to those that did not have intentions to migrate (40 percent versus 19 percent) (figure 2.5). They were also more likely to report wage-income losses and needing to use drastic coping mechanisms such as cutting food spending due to lack of income. This vulnerable group also faces higher health concerns, with more COVID-related symptoms, mental health issues, and higher chances of not receiving the necessary health treatment.

FIGURE 2.5

**Impact of COVID-19 on the economic and health outcomes of families with cancelled migration plans**

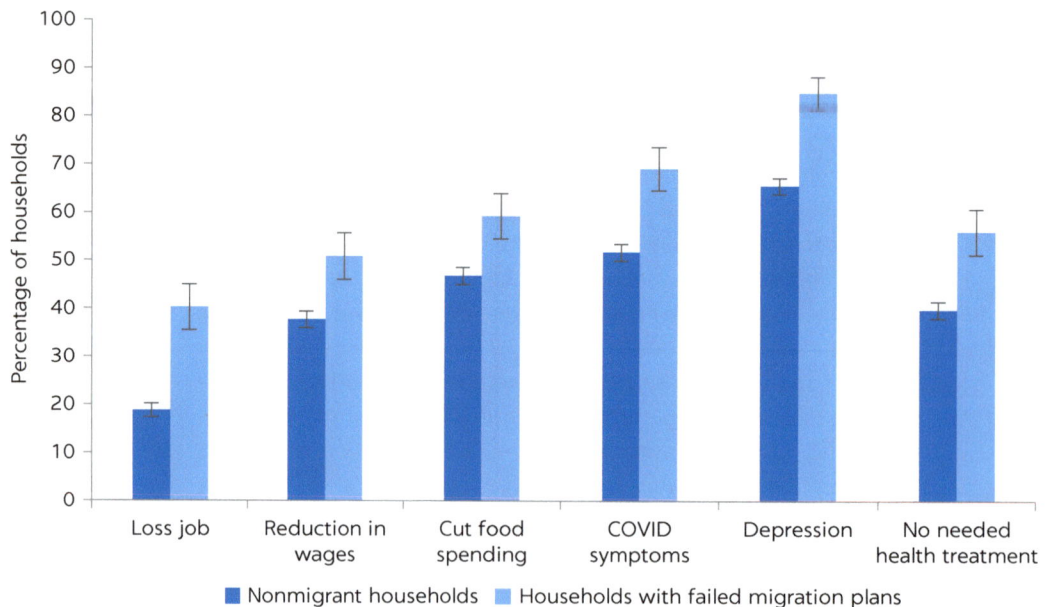

Source: National Statistical Committee household survey 2020.

## DURING MIGRATION

### COVID-19 health risks

Migrants abroad have been exposed to significant health risks compared to the nonmigrant population in the Kyrgyz Republic. There are no official and publicly available data on COVID-19 infections or mortality rates specifically among migrants in main destination countries such as the Russian Federation or Kazakhstan. However, there are several reasons to believe that their health exposure to COVID-19 has been higher than that of nonmigrants in the Kyrgyz Republic. First, the COVID-19 prevalence in the Russian Federation, the main destination country, has been more than double that in the Kyrgyz Republic. In addition, migrants in the Russian Federation were more exposed to health risks than Russian citizens given their particular legal, economic, and social vulnerabilities and the barriers they faced to get access to COVID-19 tests and medical health care in case of having symptoms (King and Zotova 2020). Furthermore, the housing conditions of Kyrgyz migrants tend to be less amenable for social distancing, with about half of Kyrgyz migrants living in apartments with more than five other people (4.5 on average), compared to only 15 percent of Russians (Varshaver, Ivanova, and Rocheva 2020). This hinders the ability to self-quarantine in case of contraction of COVID-19 (King and Zotova 2020). Finally, the substandard living conditions in nonresidential buildings (such as abandoned factories, basements, or trailers) lack basic amenities, which also increases the risks of health hazards, in particular respiratory illnesses (Centre for Migration Research 2014). Under these circumstances there have been frequent outbreaks among migrant groups reported in the media.[2]

### Exposure to employment shocks at destination

In the absence of nationally representative surveys of migrants abroad during the peak of COVID-19,[3] the analysis of occupations prior to the onset of the pandemic provides a relevant approximation of the vulnerability of employment to the COVID-19 crisis. Recent studies have estimated individual ex ante job vulnerability to COVID-19 based on the characteristics of the jobs (see, for example, Dingel and Neiman 2020; Garrote-Sanchez et al. 2020). Using ONET surveys that provide information on the task content of occupations, the KIHS migration module of 2015, and the general KIHS survey in 2018, we categorized jobs as "income-safe" if they are jobs that can be performed from home (teleworkable) or are deemed essential by governments, so they are protected from supply restrictions in mobility and dismissals (Fasani and Mazza 2020).

Kyrgyz migrants hold jobs in occupations that were more vulnerable to the COVID-19 shock than nonmigrants. Panels a and b of figure 2.6 highlight several important results. In general, mid-educated workers (completed secondary education) are the most likely to be employed in essential occupations, while the ability to work from home increases with the level of education. When combining the two aspects of protection against COVID-19 in the labor market, higher-educated workers tend to have a larger share of jobs that are safer from dismissal and income losses (panel c). By migration status, while 64 percent of nonmigrant workers in the Kyrgyz Republic were employed in income-safe jobs, only 46 percent of emigrants were employed in these types of jobs. Therefore, Kyrgyz emigrants are significantly more vulnerable to supply and

FIGURE 2.6

**Exposure to COVID-19 employment shocks, by migration status**

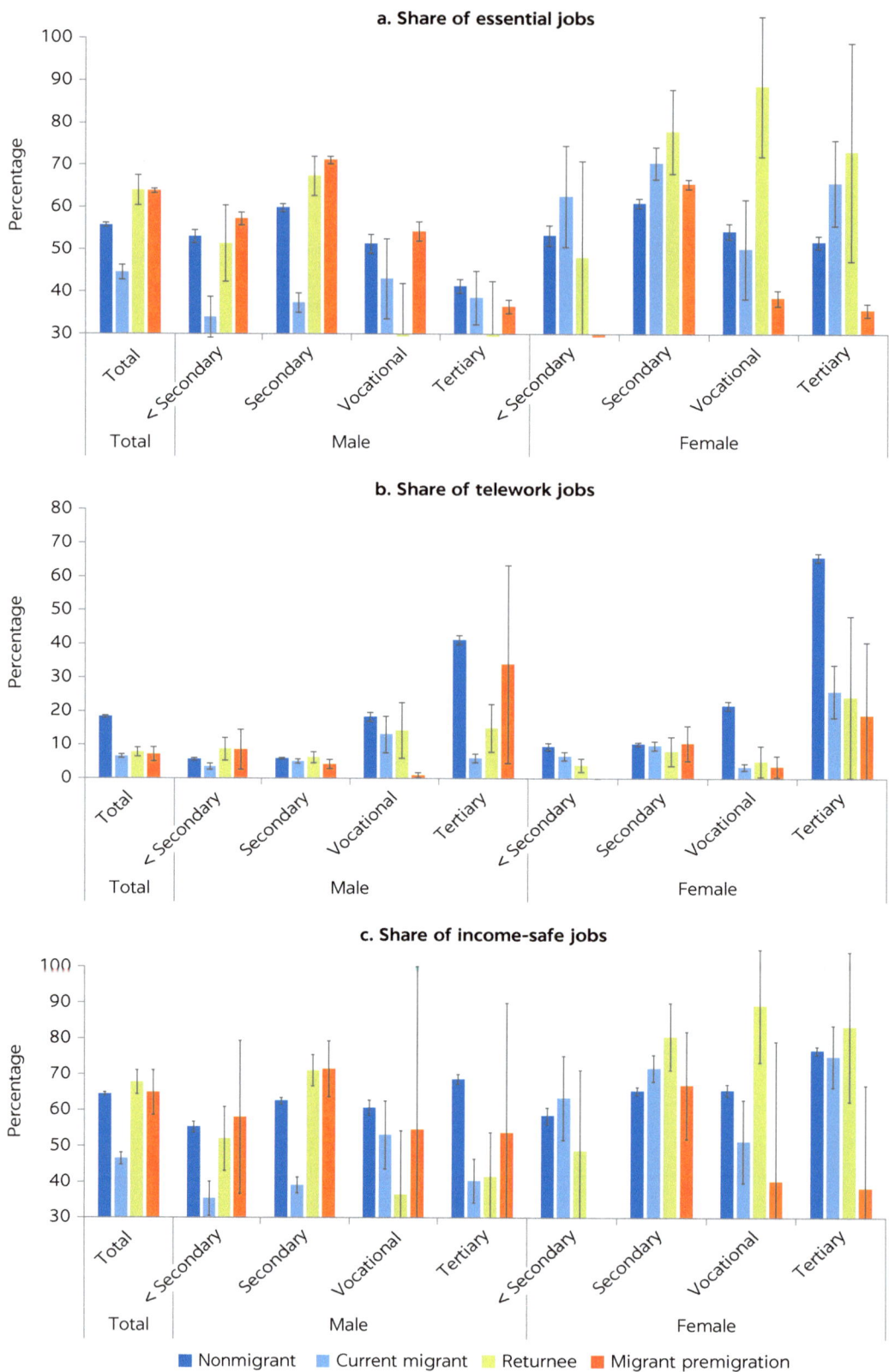

a. Share of essential jobs

b. Share of telework jobs

c. Share of income-safe jobs

Nonmigrant    Current migrant    Returnee    Migrant premigration

Sources: World Bank, based on data from the KIHS annual survey and ad hoc migration module (2015) and following the methodology of Dingel and Neiman (2020), and Fasani and Mazza (2020).

demand constraints in the labor market in sending countries (mainly the Russian Federation). Emigrants are not only employed in more vulnerable occupations compared to nonmigrants, but also relative to their former occupations before migrating. This increase in vulnerability between migrants and nonmigrants is particularly large for emigrants with higher education levels.

Surveys of migrants in the Russian Federation corroborate the larger negative impact of COVID-19 on the labor market outcomes of this population group, compared to both native Russians and nonmigrants in the Kyrgyz Republic. Several surveys conducted in the Russian Federation found that Kyrgyz and migrants from other Central Asian countries experienced large employment losses in the first two months of the pandemic (Varshaver, Ivanova, and Rocheva 2020; Ryazantsev and Khramova 2020; Denisenko and Mukomel 2020). According to Varshaver, Ivanova, and Rocheva (2020) about 40 percent of Kyrgyz migrants lost their jobs during the first two months of the pandemic, and an additional 39 percent were sent to unpaid leave. Therefore, only one in five Kyrgyz migrants was able to keep earning wages. As a comparison, about 40 percent of Russians were either dismissed or on unpaid leave during the same period. Other surveys of Central Asian migrants show similar results. Ryazantsev and Khramova (2020) find that 28 percent of migrants lost their job and 37 percent were on unpaid leave, and Denisenko and Mukomel (2020) report a 30 percent drop in employment of migrants in April and May of 2020 compared to February of the same year. In consonance with the fall in employment, Varshaver, Ivanova, and Rocheva (2020) find that only 15 percent of Kyrgyz migrants maintained their levels of pre-COVID-19 labor earnings. The partial economic recovery in the Russian Federation in the second half of 2020 given the lower mobility restrictions suggests that part of the migrants' job loss could have been restored (Ryazantsev and Khramova 2020), but there are no recent data on the labor market outcomes of Kyrgyz migrants in the Russian Federation. In the second half of 2021, when the economic situation had already improved, the L2CK shows that 64 percent of Kyrgyz migrants in the Russian Federation were employed, still significantly lower rates than premigration levels when temporary migrants were almost universally employed.

The impact of COVID-19 on employment of Kyrgyz migrants in the Russian Federation has been unequal across regions and sectors of activity. Employment losses among labor migrants in the Russian Federation were significantly higher in the Moscow metropolitan area (41 percent compared to 21 percent in other areas of the country), partly due to the stricter mobility restrictions imposed there (Denisenko and Mukomel 2020). Across types of labor migrants, the negative shock was particularly acute among migrants with informal contracts, lower education levels, and limited Russian language fluency (Denisenko and Mukomel 2020). In line with the ex ante analysis of vulnerabilities to COVID-19 based on occupations, the different surveys show large variations in employment losses across sectors. According to Ryazantsev and Khramova (2020), the sectors where labor migrants were strongly hit were tourism, hospitality, hairdressing, and retail trade (see figure 2.7). Employment in construction, the largest employer of labor migrants, fell by 30 percent, although Denisenko and Mukomel (2020) show that it recovered in May 2020. On the other hand, the share of migrants that lost their job in the health care, utilities, and delivery sectors was minimal. In some instances, there has been an increase

FIGURE 2.7

**Share of employment losses among labor migrants in the Russian Federation across economic sectors**

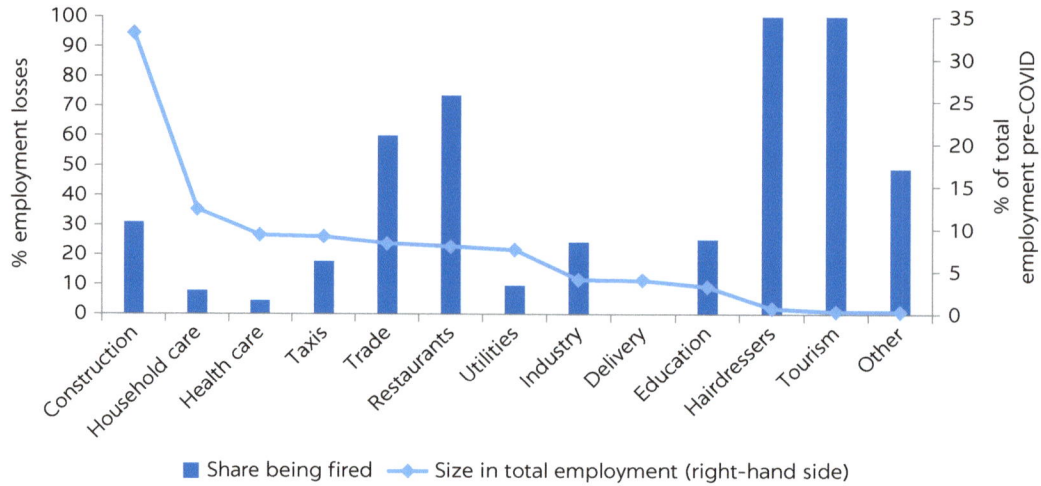

*Source:* Ryazantsev and Khramova (2020).

in demand for home services, courier delivery, utilities (yardmen, disinfectors), and cleaning services. In the medium term, the recovery of the Russian economy seems to be accompanied by important sectoral shifts, so it is important for labor migrants to be able to adjust their skills to the sectors most in demand.

## Migrants' lack of access to employment protection and social assistance

Part of the reason why the drop in employment during COVID-19 was more acute among Kyrgyz migrants than the native population is the higher degree of informality. Prior to the COVID-19 outbreak, more than one in five Kyrgyz emigrants in the Russian Federation and Kazakhstan had a verbal contract with their employer or other informal arrangements as opposed to any written contract in compliance with the national labor laws (figure 2.8). These types of agreements, which are more prevalent among migrants with low education levels, limit the labor protection of workers, which is particularly harmful when large negative shocks to the economy like the COVID-19 pandemic hit. In 2018, only a minority of emigrants benefited from social security benefits (13 percent) or paid leave (18 percent) or had furlough mechanisms of mandatory temporary leave instead of layoffs (12 percent). This contrasts with a close to universal access in the Kyrgyz Republic (93 percent, 89 percent, and 87 percent, respectively). It is not a surprise that surveys carried out during the COVID-19 pandemic such as Ryazantsev and Khramova (2020) find that only a very small minority of migrants in the Russian Federation received social protection from their employer or Russian authorities (3.5 percent) when the pandemic hit. As a result, Kyrgyz migrants faced a very dire economic situation, with only 28 percent of respondents in the survey by Vershaver, Ivanova, and Rocheva (2020) having savings to survive without income for more than a month (and only 9 percent for more than 3 months). The main challenges migrants reported was

**FIGURE 2.8**

**Type of contract and legal protection of Kyrgyz migrants and nonmigrants**

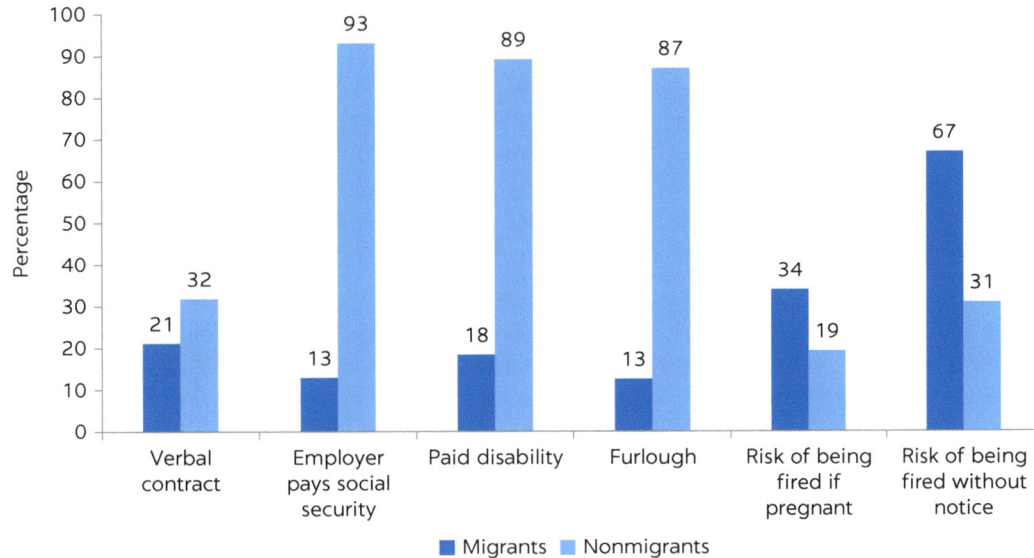

*Source:* Kyrgyz Republic Integrated Household Survey (2018).

the inability to pay rent (64 percent) and pay for food (43 percent) (Ryazantsev and Khramova 2020). Similarly, a study by IOM and UNICEF (2020) of Kyrgyz families with migrants abroad highlighted the need of food and essential supplies as the largest concern of two in five respondents. Kyrgyz emigrant workers were also significantly more likely than Kyrgyz in the Kyrgyz Republic to report fears of being fired without due notice (67 percent compared to 31 percent) and for reasons such as being pregnant (34 percent compared to 19 percent). Migrants also faced barriers to accessing formal grievance redress mechanisms to file complaints when their labor rights were not met, increasing the risks of abuses (Kyrgyz Integrated Household Survey 2018). Therefore, once the pandemic hit and companies had to let workers go, Kyrgyz emigrants were easier to be dismissed given their low employment protection.

Not only Kyrgyz migrants' jobs were hit hard, but they also had limited access to social protection programs while abroad to weather the negative COVID-19 shock. Kyrgyz labor migrants usually fall through the cracks of social protection systems in both receiving countries (for example the Russian Federation, Kazakhstan) and the Kyrgyz Republic. In the Kyrgyz Republic, social protection spending is similar to other benchmark countries in the region (figure 2.9). Social insurance accounts for the bulk of the Kyrgyz Republic's social protection spending, in particular old age retirement pensions, while spending on labor market policies is very low. However, labor emigrants are still unable to contribute to the Kyrgyz social assistance system. This poses a longer-term threat to the fiscal sustainability of the Kyrgyz pension system (OECD 2018). In host countries, even within the EaEU, many Kyrgyz emigrants do not have de facto legal protection (box 2.2) nor do they have similar access to services such as health care or unemployment benefits as natives (Sharifzoda 2019). As the Kyrgyz Integrated Household Survey of 2018 shows, only 13 percent of Kyrgyz workers abroad benefit from social security benefits. Overall, Kyrgyz migrant workers are mostly

## The legal protection of Kyrgyz migrants in main destination countries

The legal protection of Kyrgyz migrants in the two main destination countries (the Russian Federation and Kazakhstan) has been strengthened since the country's accession to the Eurasian Economic Union (EaEU) on August 6, 2015.[4] The founding treaty enshrines the free movement of labor across member states as one of the founding principles. As a result, Kyrgyz migrants in the Russian Federation do not need to comply with the patent system created for migrants from other countries such as Tajikistan or

Uzbekistan. However, Article 96 of the EaEU treaty defines employment as "activities performed under an employment contract or in execution of works (services) under a civil law contract carried out on the territory of the state of employment in accordance with the legislation of that state." This narrow definition still leaves many Kyrgyz migrants that do not have a formal contract with a Russian or Kazakh employer unprotected and maintains vulnerabilities in their legal status.

FIGURE 2.9

**Social protection expenditures as a share of GDP, 2015**

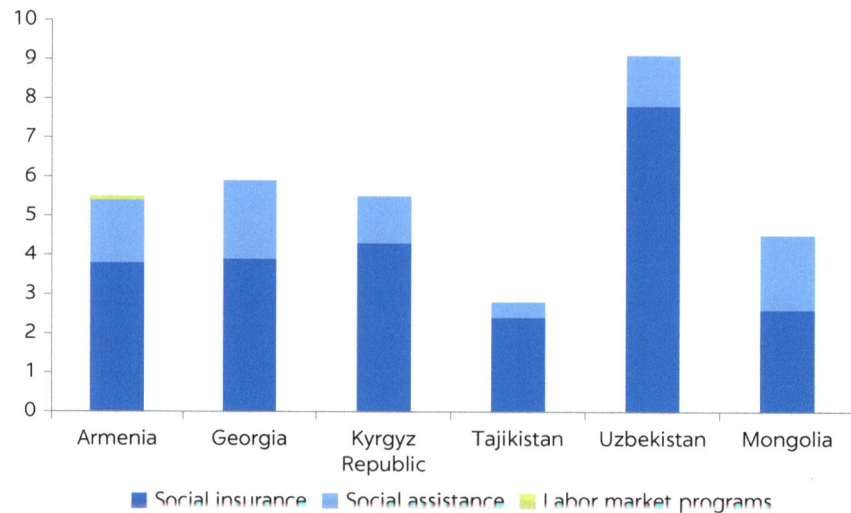

*Source:* Social Protection Indicator, Asia Development Bank.

excluded from accessing social protection programs either in their own country or abroad, which makes them and their families particularly vulnerable to negative income or health shocks that could push them into poverty. The COVID-19 pandemic has put the vulnerabilities of emigrants in the Russian Federation or other receiving countries at the forefront in terms of their insufficient access to social protection in the labor market. Given the status quo of informality and limited social protection, many migrants working abroad lost their jobs without receiving any compensation or protection (Kuznetsova et al. 2020). In the case of contracting the virus, Kyrgyz emigrants lacked proper access to health care and were more exposed to layoffs if they required sick leave. The lack of social protection of Kyrgyz emigrants has had dramatic consequences during the pandemic, with a vast majority struggling to obtain enough funding to pay basic expenditures such as rent and food (Ryazantsev and Khramova 2020).

## RETURN MIGRATION

The COVID-19 pandemic had countervailing effects on returns, with international mobility restrictions limiting return flows while low employment opportunities in host countries incentivized them. Many migrants who wanted to return home could not do so because of the closure of frontiers and lack of international flights. According to the Listening to the Citizens of the Kyrgyz Republic survey of 2021, the upward trend in the share of return migrants arriving observed in previous years came to an halt in 2020 (panel a of figure 2.10), due to the almost nonexistent return in the first three months of the pandemic (April to June of 2020) (panel b of figure 2.10). More strikingly, 8 percent of Kyrgyz households in the National Statistical Committee Household Survey of 2020 reported having a member overseas who was unable to return home, the equivalent of 128,000 households (and at minimum that figure of current emigrants).

**FIGURE 2.10**

**Number of return migrants to the Kyrgyz Republic**

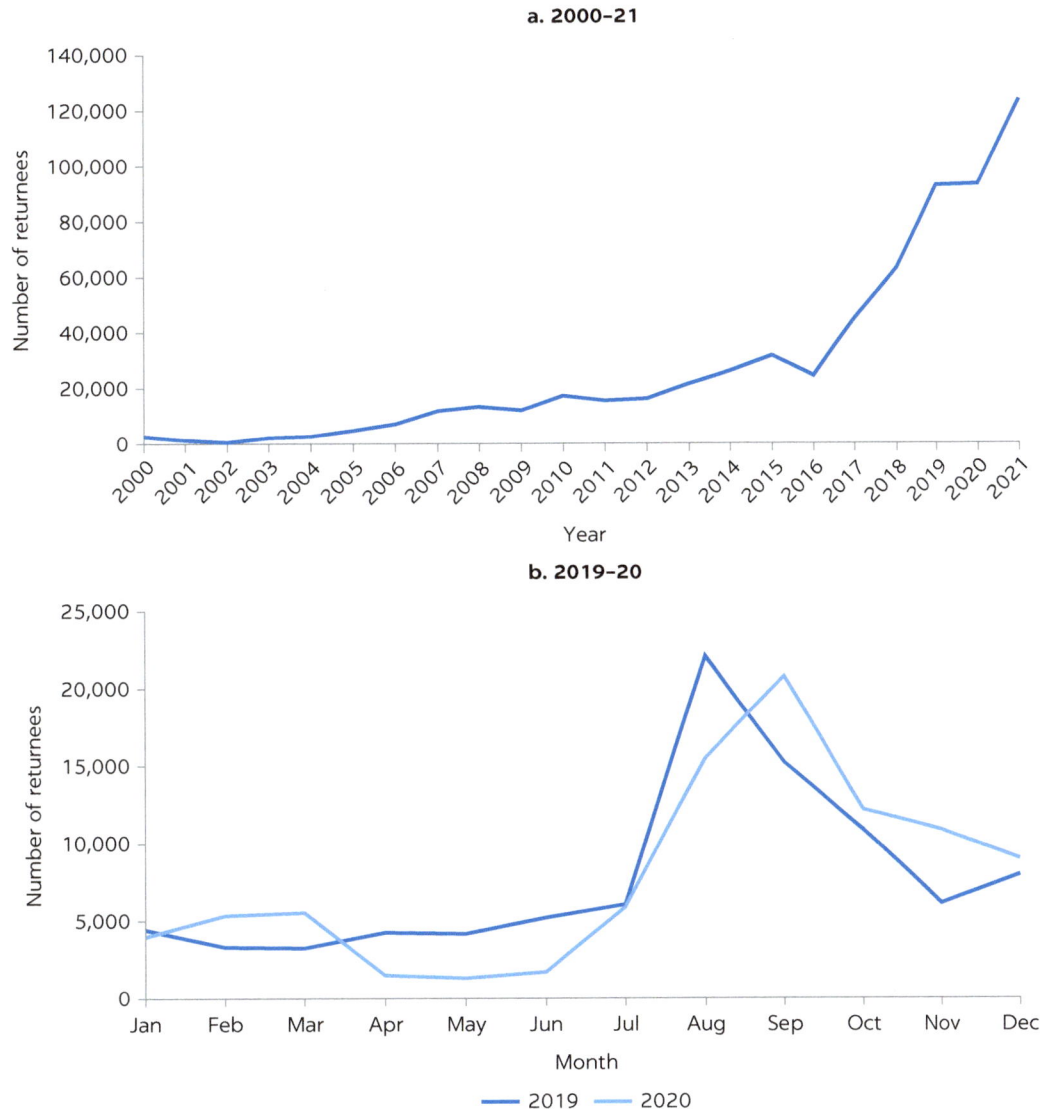

Source: Listening to the Citizens of the Kyrgyz Republic (2021).

Interestingly, households reporting having a member stranded abroad tend to have higher income levels, most likely due to the larger size of international remittances received. The high number of Kyrgyz migrants that intended to return but were not able to do so based on statistics in the Kyrgyz Republic contrast with surveys in the Russian Federation that show a much lower willingness to return home in the first months of the pandemic despite the economic hardship. Denisenko and Mukomel (2020) found that three in four migrants did not plan to leave the Russian Federation in the coming six months, while Ryazantsev and Khramova (2020) estimated this ratio to be about two in three. The discrepancies could be due to the fact that surveys in the Russian Federation included mostly migrants from Uzbekistan and Tajikistan, countries that, as opposed to the Kyrgyz Republic, are not part of the Eurasian Economic Union, hindering the ability to remigrate. As such, migrants from these countries might be less mobile and unwilling to return home in response to negative shocks, given the higher cost and barriers to obtain further documents to emigrate to the Russian Federation.

As mobility restrictions have eased, many migrants have returned to the Kyrgyz Republic, given limited employment opportunities in destination countries. In 2021, the pace of return migration resumed its upward trend (panel a of figure 2.10) fueled by both the return of stranded migrants and of new emigrants who migrated during 2021. The survey on the impact of the COVID-19 pandemic implemented by the National Statistics Committee (2020) estimates that 5 percent of Kyrgyz households had at least one member who lost their job overseas and were forced to return to the Kyrgyz Republic (figure 2.11, panel a), which is equivalent to 76,862 returnees or more (depending on the number of return migrants per household). Statistics from the Ministry of Foreign Affairs collected by the different embassies reported about 50,000 returnees by the end of the summer, and the State Migration Services

**FIGURE 2.11**

**Share of households with disrupted migration plans**

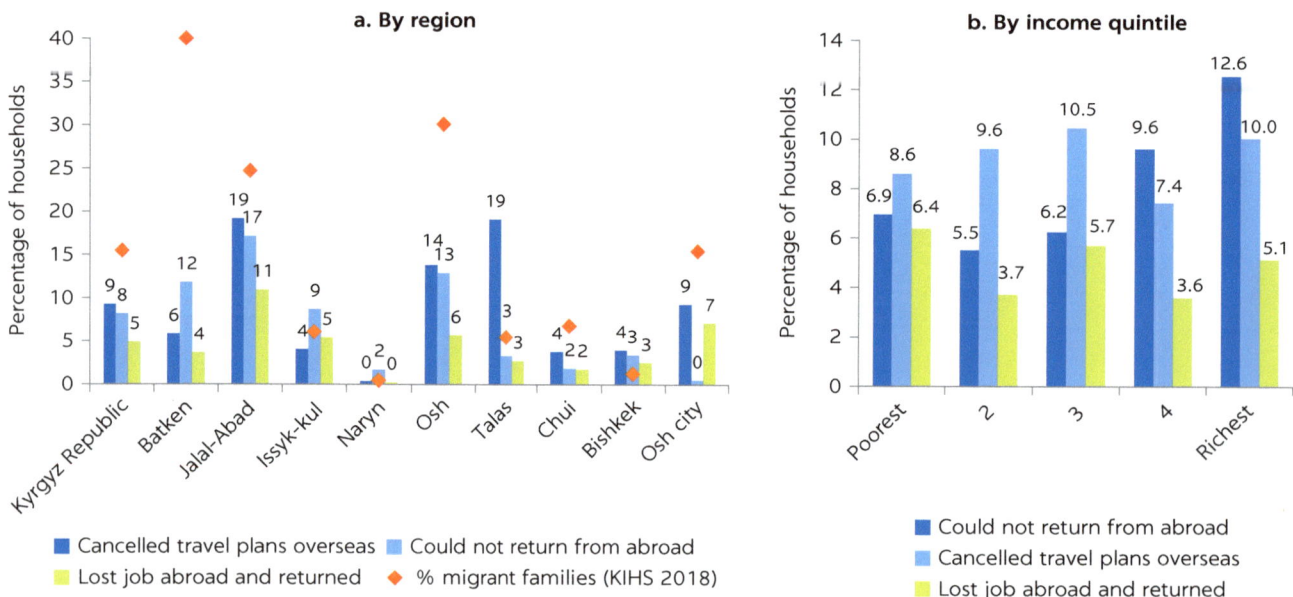

*Sources:* National Statistics Committee (2020) and Kyrgyz Integrated Household Survey (2018).

expected the number to reach 100,000, in line with estimates from the National Statistics Committee survey of October 2020. Actual observed returns from the L2CK show a total number of 78,000 returns between April and December of 2021.

The integration of returnees after large negative shocks like COVID-19 can be particularly challenging given the limited absorptive capacity of the Kyrgyz labor market. The ex ante measures of vulnerability in the labor market reported previously in this chapter show a similar level of exposure to the income-related shock for returnees vis-à-vis nonmigrants, given that the lower presence in teleworkable occupations is compensated with a higher propensity to be employed in essential occupations (in particular in the agriculture sector). However, the limited employment opportunities in the context of the COVID-19 pandemic, the large number of return migrants and the particular barriers that some of them might face when navigating local labor markets—with potentially lower networks and knowledge of the bureaucratic processes—suggests that they might be a particularly vulnerable group. When surveying migrants from Central Asia that returned from the Russian Federation after the COVID-19 outbreak, Denisenko and Mukomel (2020) found that only 40 percent of them worked by early June 2020. The 2020 National Statistics Committee COVID-19 survey also shows a higher degree of economic and health vulnerability among households with members who were either forced to return or were stranded and could not return from abroad. While less than 20 percent of nonmigrant households reported having members that lost their job during the pandemic, the rate reached 33 percent for households with a migrant who was stranded, and 54 percent for households with a member who had to return to the Kyrgyz Republic (figure 2.12). Households with recent returnees not only were more likely than nonmigrant families to see a reduction in wage income since the start of the pandemic, but also in remittances, which represent an increasing share of income for migrant

**FIGURE 2.12**

**Impact of COVID-19 on economic and health outcomes of households with or without a past or current migrant**

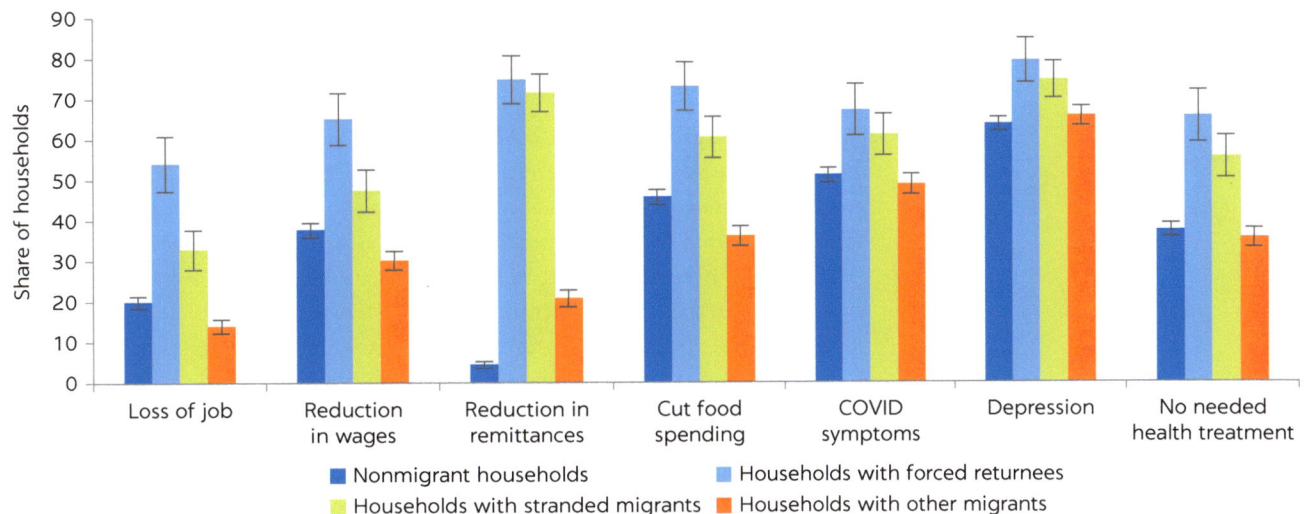

*Source:* National Statistical Committee household survey 2020.

families. Given the larger negative shock that families with returnees face, they were also significantly more likely to report using strategies such as cutting food spending to cope with the lower income. Healthwise, households with recent returnees also had a higher incidence of COVID-19-related symptoms and mental health issues, and were more likely to be left without the necessary health treatment.

## IMPACTS ON MIGRANT HOUSEHOLD MEMBERS AND THE HOME ECONOMY

The global nature of the COVID-19 crisis has defied the historical counter-cyclical trends in remittance flows. The COVID-19 crisis has simultaneously hit sending and receiving countries, with ambiguous effects on remittances. On the one hand, migrants remit more when the needs of relatives and friends in the country of origin are higher (Gupta 2005). However, remittances are impacted by the number of emigrants and their ability to remit based on their savings and earnings (Clemens and McKenzie 2018). Given the reduction in the stock of Kyrgyz emigrants and their high income-exposure to COVID-19, remittance inflows to the Kyrgyz Republic saw their largest drops in recent history, with a year-on-year fall of more than 50 percent in the month of April (panel a of figure 2.13). However, remittances had bounced back since the summer of 2020, and the cumulative flows by October 2020 were only 2.3 percent lower than in the same month of 2019 (panel b of figure 2.13). In light of the continuing reduction of Kyrgyz emigrants to the Russian Federation until the third quarter of 2020 and the still-dire labor market situation in receiving countries, the rebound in remittances suggests a higher elasticity of foreign earnings to remittances of emigrants, perhaps financed by previous savings, in an increased effort to support the larger needs of household members in the Kyrgyz Republic.

At the household level, surveys show a widespread reduction in remittances in the first months of the pandemic, which had a severe negative impact on the welfare of migrant households. In the Russian Federation, Ryazantsev and Khramova (2020) found that 79 percent of migrants who used to send remittances stopped sending any money by the end of April 2020, very similar to the drop in remittances observed at the macro level during that month. In the Kyrgyz Republic, the National Statistics Committee survey in October 2020 shows that 16 percent of Kyrgyz households experienced a reduction in the amount of remittances received. Given that around 20 percent of Kyrgyz households were receiving remittances before the pandemic (KIHS 2018), this means that four in five households receiving remittances saw their income from this source reduced. Households with a family member abroad are particularly reliant on this source of income. The reduction in remittances affects households in the highest income quintiles (figure 2.14, panel a). However, as shown in this chapter, given the high dependency on this source of income among migrant families, a severe reduction in remittances could cause a rapid increase in poverty rates for these households. At the regional level, regions with a higher drop in remittances also reported higher overall income losses (figure 2.14, panel b), highlighting the role of remittances as a key source of income. Households that suffered a loss in remittances after the pandemic were more likely to resort to coping strategies such as cutting food spending,

**FIGURE 2.13**

**Recent trends in remittances to the Kyrgyz Republic, 2016–21**

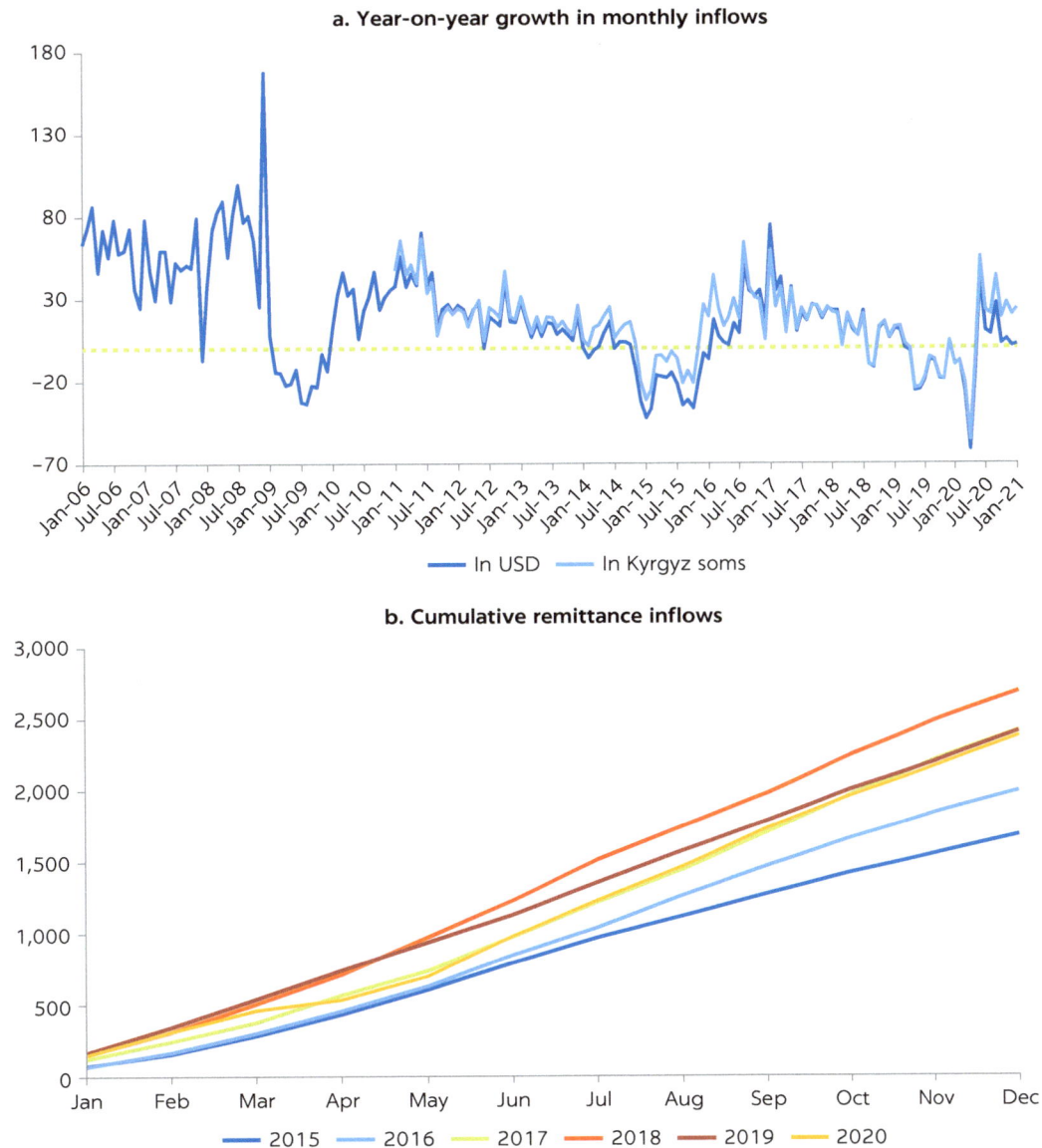

**a. Year-on-year growth in monthly inflows**

In USD — In Kyrgyz soms

**b. Cumulative remittance inflows**

— 2015 — 2016 — 2017 — 2018 — 2019 — 2020

*Source:* National Bank of the Kyrgyz Republic.

not paying utilities, using savings, or requesting a loan to compensate for the loss of income (table 2.1). These results hold even after controlling for region (oblast) of residence, household size, self-reported poverty, or changes in employment or wage earnings.

It is unclear how the decline in labor migration linked to COVID-19 influenced labor force participation rates of migrant households. As discussed, descriptive evidence for the Kyrgyz Republic suggests a negative correlation between having a household member overseas and the labor force participation of members staying behind. Global evidence on this issue is mixed, although most studies find that inflows of remittances reduce labor participation of migrant households (OECD 2018). At the same time, the OECD (2018) suggests that women left behind compensate for the absence of a male

**FIGURE 2.14**

## Share of households with reductions in remittances, by income quintile and region

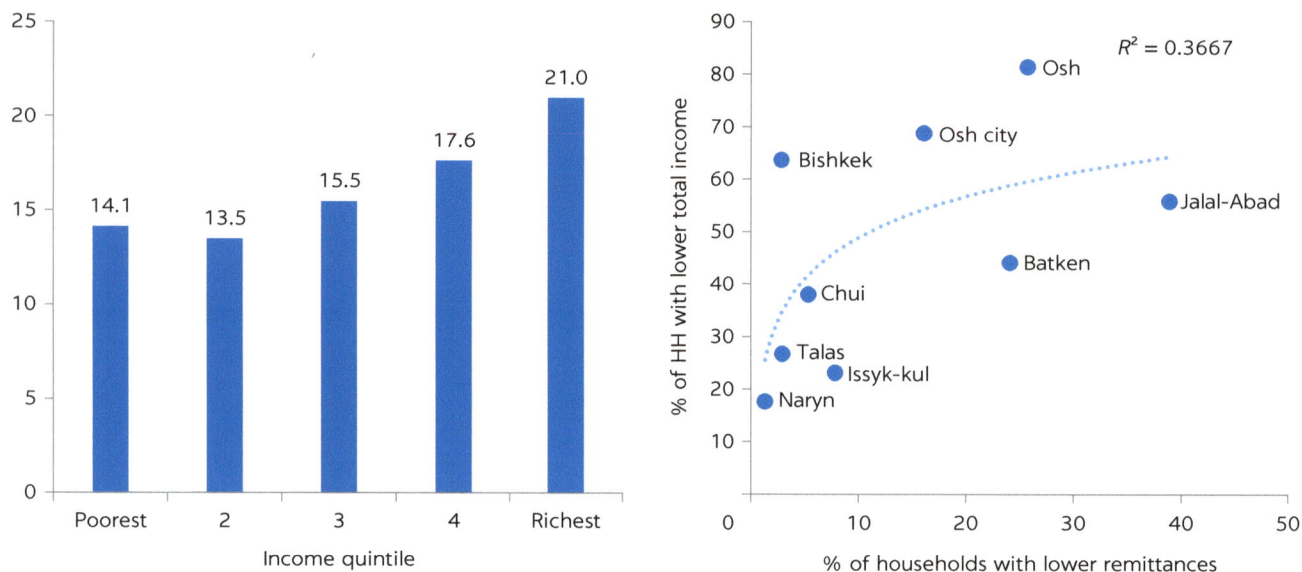

*Source:* National Statistics Committee (2020).

**TABLE 2.1 Impact of a reduction in remittances on coping strategies**

| VARIABLE | (1) CUT FOOD SPENDING | (2) DID NOT PAY UTILITIES | (3) USED SAVINGS | (4) REQUESTED A LOAN | (5) COULD NOT AFFORD NECESSARY HEALTH CARE |
|---|---|---|---|---|---|
| Lost job | 0.230*** | 0.220*** | 0.130*** | 0.206*** | 0.109*** |
|  | (0.024) | (0.027) | (0.025) | (0.028) | (0.029) |
| Loss wages | 0.187*** | 0.079*** | 0.185*** | 0.093*** | 0.007 |
|  | (0.023) | (0.023) | (0.023) | (0.022) | (0.024) |
| Loss remittances | 0.105*** | 0.071*** | 0.183*** | 0.095*** | 0.154*** |
|  | (0.026) | (0.024) | (0.026) | (0.024) | (0.028) |
| Household size | 0.009** | 0.006 | 0.007 | 0.006 | 0.011** |
|  | (0.004) | (0.004) | (0.004) | (0.004) | (0.005) |
| Poor | 0.207*** | 0.196*** | -0.002 | 0.239*** | 0.040 |
|  | (0.028) | (0.030) | (0.034) | (0.033) | (0.034) |
| Constant | 0.151*** | 0.010 | 0.291*** | 0.255*** | 0.146*** |
|  | (0.024) | (0.020) | (0.028) | (0.026) | (0.026) |
| Observations | 4,954 | 4,954 | 4,954 | 4,954 | 4,954 |
| $R^2$ | 0.272 | 0.270 | 0.183 | 0.180 | 0.125 |
| Oblast FE | YES | YES | YES | YES | YES |

*Note:* Regression analysis with robust standard errors in parentheses.
*** $p<0.01$, ** $p<0.05$, * $p<0.1$.

household member (who migrated) with their labor, especially in the event of no remittances. Thus, one might expect the labor force participation of household members staying behind to increase as a result of the pandemic, although evidence to support this is still thin.

## NOTES

1. See Garrote-Sanchez et al. (2021) for a review of the literature on the labor market impact of COVID-19 in other countries.
2. See, for example, https://lenta.ru/news/2020/04/15/sto_migrantov/.
3. The Listening to the Citizens of the Kyrgyz Republic survey provides information on employment outcomes of migrants during the summer/autumn of 2021, when economic activity had already partially recovered.
4. Currently, the EaEU is composed of five countries: Armenia, Belarus, Kazakhstan, the Kyrgyz Republic, and the Russian Federation.

## REFERENCES

Ahmed, S. A., and L. Bossavie. 2022. "Towards Safer and More Productive Migration for South Asia." World Bank, Washington, DC. https://openknowledge.worldbank.org /handle/10986/37444.

Auer, D., F. Römer, and J. Tjaden. 2020. "Corruption and the Desire to Leave: Quasi-Experimental Evidence on Corruption as a Driver of Emigration Intentions." *IZA Journal of Development and Migration* 11 (1): 7.

Bah, T. L., and C. Batista. 2018. "Understanding Willingness to Migrate Illegally: Evidence from a Lab in the Field Experiment." NOVA Working Paper 1803.

Centre for Migration Research. 2014. "Защита прав москвичей в условиях массовой миграции." Moscow. http://www.hse.ru/pubs/lib/data/access/ram/ticket/42/1440070295402d2ca1 dc001712b71dba8c b6884c44/Blok.pdf.

Clemens, M., E. Lewis, and H. Postel. 2018. "Immigration Restrictions as Active Labor Market Policy: Evidence from the Mexican Bracero Exclusion." *American Economic Review* 108 (6): 1468–87.

Clemens, M. A., and D. McKenzie. 2018. "Why Don't Remittances Appear to Affect Growth?" *Economic Journal* 128 (612): F179–F209.

Denisenko, M., and V. Mukomel. 2020. "Labor Migration During the Corona Crisis." Institute of Demography and the Institute of Sociology FSRC RAS, June.

Dingel, J., and B. Neiman. 2020. "How Many Jobs Can be Done at Home?" *Journal of Public Economics* 189 (September): 104235.

Dzushupov, K., E. Lucero-Prisno, D. Vishnyakov, X. Lin, and A. Ahmadi. 2021. "COVID-19 in Kyrgyzstan: Navigating a Way Out." *Journal of Global Health* 11: 03020.

Fasani, F., and J. Mazza. 2020. "Immigrant Key Workers: Their Contribution to Europe's COVID-19 Response." IZA Policy Paper 155.

Garrote-Sanchez, D., N. Gomez-Parra, C. Özden, and B. Rijkers. 2020. "Which Jobs Are Most Vulnerable to COVID-19? What an Analysis of the European Union Reveals." World Bank Research and Policy Brief 148384.

Gupta, P. 2005. "Macroeconomic Determinants of Remittances: Evidence from India." IMF Working Paper 05/224.

IOM (International Organization for Migration) and UNICEF. 2020. "Rapid Needs Assessment of the Challenges Facing Migrant Workers and Their Families Impacted by the Covid-19 Outbreak." A study based on the surveys of Kyrgyz labor migrants and members of their families left behind and NGO representatives.

Kuznetsova, I, R. Mogilevskii, A. Murzakulova, A. Abdoubaetova, A. Wolters, and J. Round. 2020. "Migration and COVID-19: Challenges and Policy Responses in the Kyrgyz Republic." CAP paper 247 (December), Central Asia Program.

McKenzie, D., J. Gibson, and S. Stillman. 2013. "A Land of Milk and Honey with Streets Paved with Gold: Do Emigrants Have Over-Optimistic Expectations About Incomes Abroad?" *Journal of Development Economics* 102: 116–27.

National Statistical Committee. 2020. "The Impact of the COVID-19 Pandemic on Households." Government of the Kyrgyz Republic.

OECD (Organisation for Economic Co-operation and Development). 2018. "Social Protection System Review of Kyrgyzstan." OECD Development Pathways, OECD Publishing, Paris. https://www.oecd.org/countries/kyrgyzstan/Social_Protection_System_Review _Kyrgyzstan.pdf.

Porcher, C. 2020. "Migration with Costly Information." Unpublished paper.

Ryazantsev, S., and M. Khramova. 2020. "Influence of the COVID-19 Pandemic on the Position of Migrants and Remittances in Central Asia." Institute for Socio-Political Research of the Russian Academy of Sciences.

Seshan, G., and R. Zubrickas. 2017. "Asymmetric Information about Migrant Earnings and Remittance Flows." *World Bank Economic Review* 31(1): 24–43.

Sharifzoda, K. 2019. "Central Asia's Russian Migration Puzzle: An interview with Caress Schenk." *The Diplomat*, October 11. https://thediplomat.com/2019/10/central-asias -russian-migration-puzzle.

Shrestha, M. 2020. "Get Rich or Die Tryin': Perceived Earnings, Perceived Mortality Rates, and Migration Decisions of Potential Work Migrants from Nepal," *World Bank Economic Review* 34 (1): 1–27.

State Migration Services. 2021. "Concept for the Migration Policy of the Kyrgyz Republic for 2021–2030." Government of the Kyrgyz Republic.

Russian Government. 2020. "Russia Resumes Flights with Belarus, Kazakhstan, Kyrgyzstan and South Korea." Directive 2406-r of September 20. http://government.ru/en/docs/40446/.

Vershaver, E., N. Ivanova, and A. Rocheva. 2020. "Migrants in Russia during the COVID-19 Pandemic: Survey Results." https://papers.ssrn.com/sol3/papers.cfm?abstract_id=3672397.

World Bank. 2015. "Labor Migration and Welfare in the Kyrgyz Republic (2008–2013)." Report 99771-KG, Poverty Global Practice, Europe and Central Asia Region. World Bank, Washington, DC. https://openknowledge.worldbank.org/handle/10986/22960 ?locale-attribute=es.

# 3 Policy Options to Address Challenges throughout the Migration Life Cycle

## STRENGTHENING MIGRATION SYSTEMS

Migration systems in the Kyrgyz Republic are still maturing compared to the relevance of the migration phenomenon in the country. Despite the large outflows of Kyrgyz migrants, its role in absorbing part of the "youth bulge" that cannot be accommodated by local labor markets and the vital importance of remittances to the country's macroeconomic stability, and households' livelihoods, there has been a lack of coherent, long-term migration policy in the country beyond the role of managing remittances. The State Migration Services, under the Ministry of Labor, Social Protection and Migration, leads intergovernmental cooperation in the area of labor migration. The State Migration Services only has a central office in Bishkek and a small branch in Osh, while the majority of prospective migrants and returnees reside in rural areas (for example, Batken, Jalal-Abad, and Osh provinces). The physical distance to the main beneficiaries hinders their ability to access offered services. The International Organization for Migration (IOM) in the Kyrgyz Republic also supports migrants through a network of local communities, authorities, and NGOs.

The COVID-19 pandemic has highlighted the need to strengthen institutions, frameworks, and data collection to enhance safe legal migration from the Kyrgyz Republic. The existing migration management in the Kyrgyz Republic is still lacking a centralized data system and intersectoral collaboration throughout the migration cycle—from migration plans and preparations, to support and protection during the migration experience, to the reintegration of return migrants. Migration policy has to be informed by relevant and updated data, not just statistics of border crossings for security purposes and remittances data, in order to elaborate relevant and effective mechanisms to support migrants and their families (Kuznetsova et al. 2020). Legal frameworks have yet to be developed and implemented to put at the forefront of the migration agenda a rights-based approach to protect migrants and their families. The COVID-19 pandemic has highlighted the limitations of the current migration system in protecting migrants from large negative shocks. In the absence of a holistic migration framework with predictable policies, programs to support migrants coping with the COVID-19 crisis have been fragmented and of limited scope.

Strengthening systematic data collection, monitoring, and evaluation throughout the migration life cycle is necessary in a context of sizable flows of emigrants and returnees to better understand migration dynamics and tailor services to migrants' needs. As a first step, it is necessary to centralize information from different governmental bodies—which requires interagency cooperation and data sharing—and to create a unified registry of all prospective migrants, current migrants, and returnees either at reception centers or at different points of exit or entry into the country. The registry can be a starting point in collecting data on the skills and labor market situation of Kyrgyz citizens applying for jobs overseas so they can be referred to appropriate training or premigration programs. The registry can also be a building block to facilitate the reintegration of returnees and to create monitoring systems through the adoption of harmonized sets of indicators (IOM 2018b). Different agencies could then more easily access migrants' information, avoiding duplicity of procedures and overburdening migrant returnees, while having better information to tailor services to their needs. It is essential that this process of data sharing and cooperation comply with the need to maintain migrants' privacy.

The concept for migration policy of the Kyrgyz Republic for 2021–30 provides a more cohesive framework and long-term vision of migration, but it needs to be effectively implemented. The concept is the main document in the state policy on migration issues. It recognizes migration as an unavoidable result of the demographic and socioeconomic specificities of the country, and aims at creating migration policies to stabilize flows and mitigate its negative effects while enhancing developmental benefits for migrants, their families, and the country as a whole (State Migration Services 2021). It also advocates for the centralization of a single national system of migration statistics, the diversification of migration flows, securing coverage of social services for migrants, and enhancing the interagency cooperation in migration policy. The envisioned implementation is divided in two phases: 2021–2025 and 2026–2030. An action plan is being developed for each stage, with the inclusion of measures and tools for the implementation of the concept by state bodies. However, given the concept's lack of details and guidance for implementation, these goals risk remaining untargeted and not properly secured in specific programs in the implementation phase.

Policies need to address the vulnerability of migrants throughout the migration life cycle in the context of the COVID-19 pandemic and beyond (figure 3.1). As highlighted in the previous section, the COVID-19 pandemic has affected prospective and current migrants at each stage of the migration life cycle. In the remainder of this chapter, we therefore propose policies that could be implemented predeparture, during migration, and after return to reduce the vulnerability of migrants in the context of the COVID-19 pandemic and in the longer term. Given the expected slow recovery from COVID-19, and other future and recent shocks such as the Russia-Ukraine conflict, both at home and in destination countries, the enhanced challenges faced by temporary migrants in the context of the pandemic are expected to persist in the short and medium runs. This challenging context can be used as an opportunity to strengthen the migration system and develop policies and programs that can equip the Kyrgyz Republic with the adequate tools to support to migrants—through a coherent and comprehensive labor migration policy—to be better prepared for future shocks that may affect labor migration and remittances.

A more efficient and comprehensive set of migration policies requires increasing cooperation between actors involved throughout the migration

**FIGURE 3.1**

**Stages of migration life cycle, migrants' decisions, COVID-19 disruptions, and policy options**

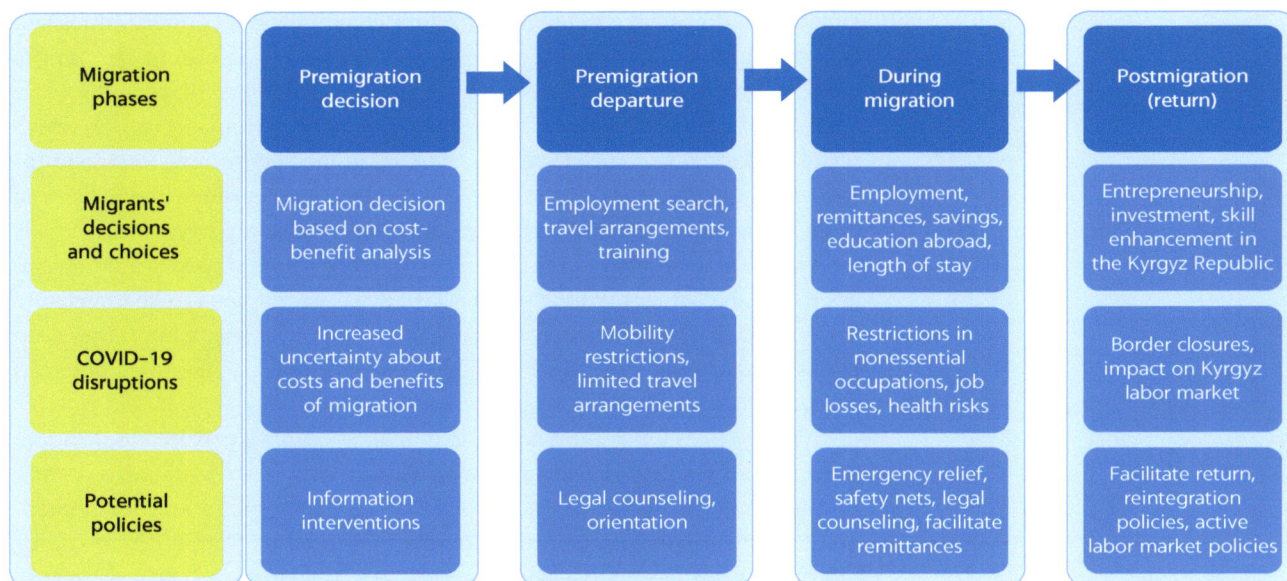

| Migration phases | Premigration decision | Premigration departure | During migration | Postmigration (return) |
|---|---|---|---|---|
| Migrants' decisions and choices | Migration decision based on cost-benefit analysis | Employment search, travel arrangements, training | Employment, remittances, savings, education abroad, length of stay | Entrepreneurship, investment, skill enhancement in the Kyrgyz Republic |
| COVID-19 disruptions | Increased uncertainty about costs and benefits of migration | Mobility restrictions, limited travel arrangements | Restrictions in nonessential occupations, job losses, health risks | Border closures, impact on Kyrgyz labor market |
| Potential policies | Information interventions | Legal counseling, orientation | Emergency relief, safety nets, legal counseling, facilitate remittances | Facilitate return, reintegration policies, active labor market policies |

*Sources:* World Bank, adapted from World Bank (2018) and Ahmed and Bossavie (2022).

life cycle. Another important area of improvement in the Kyrgyz migration system is the cooperation between all involved stakeholders, governmental and nongovernmental entities, and public and private organizations, to avoid duplicities and ensure the coherence of goals of migration and reintegration programs of different stakeholders (IOM 2018a). As previously mentioned, there is a need for a more comprehensive registry of migrants and returnees, which requires a tighter collaboration between the State Border Services (SBS)—which currently compile the only registry of people entering and leaving the country but from a security perspective—and the institutions that provide services for migrants—the State Migration Services (SMS), Ministry of Foreign Affairs (MFA), and the Ministry of Labor, Social Development and Migration (MLSDM). In the premigration phase, the migration system would benefit from a stronger supervision and regulatory framework of private employment agencies and more data sharing and coordination with MLSDM. As monitoring and support for migrants is often provided by different institutions depending on the phase of the migration life cycle (SMS during predeparture; MFA, embassies, and SMS during migration; and SMS and MLSDM upon return) the migration system would greatly benefit from an interdepartmental body to coordinate the different institutions dealing with the different phases of the migration process to avoid duplicities in bureaucratic procedures, ensure a higher level of knowledge and data sharing, and a better monitoring of migrants' journeys.

## PREDECISION AND PREDEPARTURE

Kyrgyz citizens who have to cancel their migration plans due to large negative shocks in the origin or destination country, given their forgone earning potentials and vulnerability in the domestic labor market, should be targeted by safety net programs. As shown in chapter 2, households with disrupted migration plans due to the COVID-19 pandemic have been in a particularly vulnerable economic situation in the Kyrgyz Republic, with limited employment opportunities and poorer health conditions. Access to social assistance might help smooth the adverse impacts of economic shocks on potential migrants' households while waiting to be able to migrate, and prevent their savings from drying out, which could hinder their financial ability to migrate in the near future. To target prospective migrants, it is necessary to put in place a comprehensive registry of migrants, as recommended in the previous chapter. The registry should include individuals in the premigration phase; that is, those who had plans to migrate but are still in the country. Public social assistance does not need to be targeted to households that have members with disrupted migration plans, but rather need to ensure that rural regions with a higher concentration of disrupted potential migrants are well served.

COVID-19 evidenced the need for coordination with private employment agencies and destination countries to provide up to-date-information on conditions at the destination. In the context of COVID-19, Kyrgyz authorities, in cooperation with destination countries, have an essential role to play in providing information on changes in legal restrictions to migration as well as health conditions in destination countries, so that future migrants do not need to rely on limited personal networks to obtain this key and volatile information. Prospective migrants also have higher risks of travel and employment cancellations, so legal counseling on consumer and labor rights are necessary.

More broadly, providing information about costs and benefits of migration through different platforms can increase the efficiency of migration from the Kyrgyz Republic. The concept for migration policies for 2021–30 recognizes that migrant workers leave without sufficient information about the destination country (State Migration Services 2021). Past interventions providing information to prospective migrants have been effective in aligning migrants' expectations with the realities of destination countries (Shrestha 2020) and also in increasing workers' chances of getting a job in the formal sector, as shown by Beam (2016), for the case of the Philippines. Information can be provided in different forms, such as job fairs, government premigration information programs, and through local NGOs or community leaders. Importantly, the positive impact of information interventions seems to be larger for prospective migrants with fewer networks overseas (Barsbai et al. 2020). This means that information is particularly important for low-skilled migrants who tend to have less connections, and for workers migrating to more rural areas with fewer co-nationals to rely on.

There is also a need for greater cooperation with the Russian Federation and Kazakhstan to identify skills in demand and improve the matching of Kyrgyz workers to jobs abroad. Beyond COVID-19, the Kyrgyz authorities also have a central role, in collaboration with employment agencies, in providing up-to-date information about vacant jobs in growing sectors in destination countries in the context of COVID-19 recovery and beyond, such as service delivery or agriculture. Such skill gap monitoring systems have been implemented in several destination countries such as the Republic of Korea or Malaysia for low-skilled migrants, which are then used to determine needs for migrant labor and communicated to authorities in sending countries, typically in the context of G2G agreements (Cho et al. 2018; Shrestha, Mobarak, and Sharif 2021).

Skill training for migrants is another key element for a successful migration experience when there is a mismatch between the supply of skills that migrants offer and the demand of firms in destination countries. Migrants from the Kyrgyz Republic often lack adequate skills for the jobs most in demand in the Russian Federation or Kazakhstan. Skill mismatches are partly due to occupational mobility upon migration. For example, a large portion of male migrants have an agricultural background but are hired as construction workers in the Russian Federation. Skill mismatches might have been aggravated in the context of the COVID-19 pandemic, which could have accelerated a longer-term shift in tasks and skills demanded in host labor markets. In this context, training in the skills required for employment openings in the Russian Federation would benefit all parties involved. However, prior to the crisis, the Kyrgyz Household Integrated Survey of 2018 shows that only 1 percent of prospective migrants took any work-related training courses to improve their chances to find employment overseas. The Ministry of Labor, Social Development and Migration is planning to implement different initiatives within the recently created Fund for Skill Development. One of the aims is to increase skills for migrants by training them in fields and skills that are valuable in the international labor market. Past experiences with predeparture skill upgrading programs highlight the need for a well-endowed program, prior analysis of supply and demand skill gaps, and dynamics in the destination country and at origin to tailor the content of skill trainings (IOM 2011; Global Forum on Migration and Development 2020). Cooperation with receiving countries in understanding skill gaps at destination is, thus, of high value. A particularly promising type of cross-country collaboration on skill formation are global skill partnerships (see box 3.1).

There is also a need for increasing the legal and financial literacy and migration preparedness of prospective migrants through orientation courses and training. Prospective migrants tend to come from rural and more disadvantaged backgrounds and usually lack a full understanding of migration opportunities. In many instances, migrants accept employment offers abroad in sectors in which they do not have previous experience. They are often unaware of their full labor rights and benefits given the specificities of legislation in destination countries. Premigration orientation courses for prospective migrants can provide essential

---

**BOX 3.1**

### Global skill partnerships: A potential tool to enhance migrants' skills

Global skill partnerships (GSPs) are bilateral arrangements between migrant sending and receiving countries by which the country of destination agrees to train people in the country of origin. Among the trainees, some choose to stay and increase human capital in the country of origin while others migrate to the country of destination for a given period of time. With these arrangements, countries of destination attract foreign workers with the skills they need. By training them before migration in the country of origin, costs are lower. In turn, the origin country also benefits as part of the trainees, stay in the country, increasing the supply of skills. Therefore, GSPs address the potential loss of human capital in the country of origin while preparing potential migrants with demanded skills for work in the host country (Clemens 2015). One important aspect is the early engagement of the private sector to align the training to the skills demanded in the labor market. Several pilots have been successfully implemented in the Australia–Pacific islands corridor and in Germany with Kosovo and Morocco.

information on their legal rights—in particular with respect to their labor contracts, financial literacy and planning targets for savings, and access to services at destination, as well as foreign language and soft skills that enhance the migration experience. They can also include information on health and safety and travel procedures. One of the most successful programs has been the Comprehensive Pre-Departure Education Program that the government of the Philippines runs for prospective migrants with a duration of four to six days (ILO 2013). While there has been little evaluation of such programs (McKenzie and Yang 2015), the existing evidence is suggestive of an overall positive impact. For example, financial literacy programs for migrants and their household members are very effective in increasing financial knowledge, savings, and information about remittance methods (Doi, McKenzie, and Zia 2014; Gibson, McKenzie, and Zia 2014).

The COVID-19 pandemic highlighted the need for improving the regulatory framework of private employment agencies to promote formal labor migration in the medium to long run. Private migrant employment agencies serve as the intermediary between foreign employers and prospective migrant workers. They provide key information to migrants who tend to have limited knowledge of the foreign labor market and job opportunities. However, there is a need for strengthening the regulatory framework and the outreach of employment programs to address interregional inequalities in accessing foreign job opportunities as well as ensuring an ethical and safe recruitment process that guarantees migrants' rights. To date, there has been a strong concentration of employment agencies in the main metropolitan areas, leaving rural areas unattended. The protection of migrants through the recruitment process by private agencies can be guaranteed by developing regulatory frameworks in accordance with the Private Employment Agencies Convention, 1997 (No. 181), of which the Kyrgyz Republic is not yet a signatory. Furthermore, the role of public agencies as regulators—providing clearance to foreign job opportunities and formal employment contracts—and as intermediaries to complement private employment agencies in remote areas has proved successful in other contexts. For example, a government-to-government program (G2G) between Bangladesh and Malaysia increased access to migration opportunities for those without social networks abroad (Shreshtha, Mobarak, and Sharif 2019). The EaEU treaty states that "Member States shall cooperate... to assist the organized recruitment of workers of the Member States for employment in the Member States" (article 96.1). This government-to-government cooperation to regulate the recruitment process of migrants is essential to guarantee successful management of legal labor migration and protection of migrants' rights. Therefore, the Kyrgyz Republic can either enhance the regulatory framework through bilateral agreements with the main destination countries or multilaterally by further regulating and implementing it within the framework of the EaEU treaty.

COVID-19 and now the economic crisis in the Russian Federation have exposed the vulnerability of migrants to shocks and evidenced the need for diversification of destinations to reduce volatility for migrants and the Kyrgyz economy. The Kyrgyz Republic has one of the highest concentrations of emigrant flows into a single destination country. Close to 80 percent of total Kyrgyz emigrants in 2019 resided in the Russian Federation according to UN-DESA, and statistics on short-term emigrants show an even higher concentration (over 90 percent, according to the KIHS or the Listening to the Citizens of the Kyrgyz

Republic survey). Kazakhstan, one of the other migration corridors, has a high synchronization of the economic business cycle with the Russian Federation (Jenish 2013), given their economic integration and dependence on raw materials. The high concentration of Kyrgyz migrants in few and synchronized markets exposes the country to high volatility and vulnerability to economic shocks in the Russian Federation or Kazakhstan. COVID-19 and now the economic crisis in the Russian Federation have shown that, as a result of this lack of diversification, migration and remittance flows are severely affected, resulting in significant welfare losses for Kyrgyz households and for the broader economy. For example, exchange rates fluctuated considerably in February and March 2022 after the start of the Russia-Ukraine war, with the ruble at one point falling by 32 percent against the Kyrgyz som. Recent data from the Listening to the Citizens of the Kyrgyz Republic survey show that many migrants delayed transfers due to the unfavorable change in exchange rates: the share of Kyrgyz households receiving any remittance transfer fell from 17.5 to 14.8 (–16 percent) during that period, and the value of a typical remittance transfer fell by 15 percent. In addition, migration intentions significantly declined during this period. In the Kyrgyz Republic, the share of households with a member considering migration fell from 13 to 8 percent.

To reduce the volatility of migration demand and flows, the government of the Kyrgyz Republic can explore new institutional frameworks such as bilateral labor agreements (BLAs), government-to-government (G2G) arrangements, and memoranda of understanding with other countries with a potential demand given their demographic trends or labor needs (for example, in Europe, the Gulf, Korea, or Malaysia).[1] For example, the Philippines, a country with a long tradition of emigration and with a well-developed migration system, has diversified the number of destination countries over the years by being very active in negotiating new bilateral labor agreements and by building a qualified workforce with credible credentials (Testaverde et al. 2017). Diversification of migration can also be enhanced in terms of occupations and not just countries of destination. About half of Kyrgyz male migrants work in construction and half of female migrants in the hospitality sector. This concentration increases the vulnerabilities of migrants' labor market status to shocks in host economies that affect particular sectors. While the EaEU allows Kyrgyz migrants in the Russian Federation and Kazakhstan to work in all sectors, further cooperation might be needed with these countries to fully recognize foreign credentials. This, combined with the provision of information to migrants on the types of job opportunities available in destination countries and the provision of training to prospective migrants when skill mismatches emerge with what firms demand at destination—as previously mentioned—can expand the employment opportunities available across sectors and professions.

## DURING MIGRATION

During the COVID-19 pandemic, governments in receiving countries have launched temporary measures to protect the legal vulnerability of migrants. On April 18, 2020, the government of the Russian Federation issued a decree "On temporary measures to resolve the legal status of foreign citizens and stateless persons in the Russian Federation in connection with the threat of further spread of the new coronavirus infection (COVID-19)," by which all foreigners in the country had the validity of their visa documents extended. In addition, work permit requirements and costs were removed. The executive order also included the suspension of deportations and court hearings on breaches of immigration laws (King and Zotova 2020). The time of validity of those measures was prolonged until December 15 by another decree on September 23.[2] These measures increased the legal security of migrants from non-EaEU countries such as Uzbekistan and Tajikistan, while Kyrgyz emigrants were already more protected as citizens of a member of the EaEU. Both the governments of the Russian Federation and Kazakhstan announced that migrants could have access to free medical care for COVID-19, even if they were undocumented in the case of the Russian Federation (Moroz, Shrestha, and Testaverde 2020). In the city of Moscow, the mayor declared that migrants will not be denied any medical assistance if they need it. Even during the initial period of quarantine, the Russian government imposed a moratorium on evictions for all people, including undocumented migrants.

On the Kyrgyz government side, the Ministry of Foreign Affairs, embassies (in particular the one in the Russian Federation), and the State Migration Services created a rapid response task force to manage the migrant crisis between March and July 2020. This rapid response task was carried out in cooperation with the IOM and leaders of the Kyrgyz diaspora in the Russian Federation. The Kyrgyz government allocated over US$188,000 (15 million KG soms) to support migrants abroad, out of which $127,000 was targeted to migrants in the Russian Federation, and $62,800 for migrants in the United Arab Emirates (Azattyk 2020). The funds were used to provide accommodation and food for those in need, in particular those infected with COVID-19, with severe illness, with large families, single mothers, or pregnant women. The Kyrgyz Embassy in the Russian Federation, with the help of diaspora groups, targeted the most vulnerable migrants. The IOM distributed protective supplies and provided food and accommodation for 282 migrants stranded in Russian airports (IOMb 2020; Kuznetsova et al. 2020) as well as in specific land borders such as the the Russian Federation-Kazakhstan one.

However, the reduced funding of these emergency programs limited their outreach compared to bolder plans for migrants in other countries, such as the one approved by the Philippines. Considering the high number of migrants from the Kyrgyz Republic in the Russian Federation and in other countries, the amount of funds for the support operation was insufficient to cushion the large negative shock suffered by Kyrgyz migrants. Conservative estimates based on the number of Kyrgyz emigrants at the time of the COVID-19 outbreak (about 250,000, according to the KIHS) and the share who lost their jobs or were sent into unpaid leave (about 80 percent, according to Vershaver, Ivanova, and Rocheva 2020) show that at least 200,000 Kyrgyz emigrants might have stayed during the initial months of the pandemic without any labor income. The allocation of US$188,000 would have just averaged to less than US$1 per Kyrgyz emigrant in need. According to the survey of migrants in the Russian Federation by Ryazantsev and Khramova (2020), only 1 percent received help and support from the embassies of their country, and 0.5 percent from the Russian authorities. Even access to more informal support channels, such as networks of compatriots, has been limited (5 percent). As an example of a more comprehensive support for their emigrant population, the government of the Philippines approved a cash assistance program to provide US$200 to at least 70,000 overseas Filipino workers (OFWs) whose employment was affected by the pandemic

(Moroz, Shrestha, and Testaverde 2020). The government of the Philippines also raised another 5 billion Filipino pesos to support migrant workers (US$0.1 billion). In total, COVID-19-related support for migrants accounted for 0.027 percent of GDP in the Philippines, compared to 0.002 percent of GDP in the Kyrgyz Republic (about 12 times more). Therefore, the Kyrgyz government has further scope to increase the support and protection of affected Kyrgyz emigrants, in line with other countries with more mature migration systems.

The COVID-19 pandemic has highlighted the need to integrate migrants into safety net programs, either at origin or at destination, to reduce migrants' vulnerabilities to shocks like COVID-19. In the Russian Federation, the government increased the amount of unemployment benefits,[3] and agreed to provide social services to citizens who lost their job after March 1, 2020, as well as to families with children and pensioners (Gorlin et al. 2020).[4] The Kyrgyz Government could coordinate with the Russian Federation and other migrant-receiving countries, in particular within the framework of the EaEU, to provide financial support to its citizens stranded abroad and, more broadly, to create a system where migrant workers make contributions to have equal access to unemployment benefits and health care as nationals from the countries of residency. Increasing formal employment channels will improve access to social protection systems (as the concept for migration policies for 2021–30 suggests), but specific arrangements need to be implemented beyond the legal status of employment, as currently even migrants with a legal contract barely have any social protection. The portability of social rights is a feature developed in other economic unions such as the European Union—where migrants have access to health care, social welfare, or pensions, as does any citizen from the host country—and migrants from countries in the EaEU would greatly benefit from a similar framework. The portability of pensions has been shown to not only enhance migrants' welfare but also to incentivize migrants to return home (Avato, Koettle, and Sabates-Wheeler 2010). Around the world, there are about 1,500 bilateral portability agreements. Beyond these bilateral and multilateral cooperation agreements, some sending countries have also created extensive social protection systems for their emigrant workers. Philippines is again a good example. Recruitment agencies provide life and personal accident insurance to foreign workers at no cost. Migrants also have health insurance coverage via PhilHealth and can voluntarily contribute to a pension system, which is promoted in predeparture training programs (Testaverde et al. 2017). The government also has agreements with several receiving countries by which migrants can file social security claims either at destination or with the Philippines. Indonesia made it compulsory for all migrants to obtain Indonesian Overseas Migrant Workers' Insurance that covers unexpected shocks such as illness, disability, death, repatriation, and funeral expenses (World Bank 2016).

Temporary relief programs for families in the Kyrgyz Republic with migrant members abroad could also be implemented. Migrant households heavily rely on international remittances. Almost all households with a migrant receive remittances (94 percent) that represent more than half of the annual household total income. The abrupt drop in remittances in the second quarter of 2020 due to the COVID-19 shock in the receiving countries' economies left many families without a large part of their disposable income and resulted in growing poverty. A 50 percent reduction in remittances, as observed in the month of April, could have pushed more than one in five migrant households into poverty based on simulations with data from the 2018 Kyrgyz Integrated Household Survey.

Remittances have gradually bounced back since the summer of 2020, when mobility restrictions in the Russian Federation were phased out, and more migrants were able to work and tried to compensate for the fall in remittances in previous months and the dire situation of their households in the Kyrgyz Republic. Still, remittances struggled to play their countercyclical role as the COVID-19 pandemic shock was global and affected both migrant-sending and -receiving countries, increasing the volatility of income of remittance-dependent households. This calls for the introduction of welfare policies for migrant families to counterbalance the drop and volatility of remittances.

Migrants and their families can benefit from policies to facilitate remittance flows by creating financial incentives and limiting bureaucratic barriers. While, at the macro level, remittances have recovered a large part of the drop observed in the first months of the pandemic, any interruption in the flow can be devastating for migrant families, which are in most instances strongly dependent on international remittances. In order to facilitate remittance flows, the government could consider recognizing remittance service providers as essential services if mobility restrictions are to be reintroduced and supporting remittance providers with instruments to help manage credit and liquidity risks (Moroz, Shrestha, and Testaverde 2020). Furthermore, while average commissions for remittance transactions between the Russian Federation and the Kyrgyz Republic are relatively low, further cooperation to support the digitalization of processes and to provide financial incentives to reduce further costs can be highly beneficial, in particular in the current context of liquidity constraints on migrant households and the subsequent recovery. Past evidence shows that even small reductions in transaction fees can result in large increases in remittances (Ambler, Aycinena, and Yang 2014). For example, Aycinena et al. (2010) found in a randomized field experiment in El Salvador that a US$1 reduction in the remittance transaction fee led to US$25 increases in the average amount of remittances sent per month. The provision of remittance services could be enhanced by promoting online transfers and mobile payments (through cell phones and blockchain wallets), and by exempting remittances flows from fees to promote their transfer through financial systems, enabling providers to operate in compliance with social distancing measures (Honorati, Yi, and Choi 2020). For example, Bangladesh allocated a central budget (US$361 million) to incentivize migrants to transfer money through legal financial systems; and Sri Lanka exempts remittance inflows from some regulations and taxes (Moroz, Shrestha, and Testaverde 2020).

In the longer term, there is a need to enhance the protection of Kyrgyz emigrants' legal rights through bilateral and multilateral agreements with receiving countries. Migrants would highly benefit from further dialog with the main receiving countries to increase Kyrgyz migrants' rights and to enhance formal labor migration with regular contracts, while providing alternative protection for migrants with informal contracts. The EaEU provides a unique platform to tackle this relevant issue multilaterally (see box 3.2), but bilateral agreements on this matter with other countries such as Türkiye are also necessary. In parallel, Kyrgyz emigrants would greatly benefit from an increasing role and capacity of consular sections (including the deployment of labor attachés in the main destination countries) in order to provide more efficient and accessible legal counselling to any Kyrgyz emigrant in need of it.

BOX 3.2

## The Eurasian Economic Union

The accession of the Kyrgyz Republic to the Eurasian Economic Union (EaEU) has promoted legal migration to some of the main destination countries, but members need to intensify cooperation. The EaEU founding treaty approved in 2015 establishes the free movement of labor across member states—which currently are Armenia, Belarus, Kazakhstan, the Kyrgyz Republic, and the Russian Federation (Eurasian Economic Commission 2015). Migrants from member states also benefit from the recognition of foreign credentials, as well as de-jure equal rights to social security benefits and emergency medical services, as do citizens of the host member state (Madiyev 2021). However, the EaEU enforcement mechanisms for migrants' rights remain weak, leading to gaps between de jure and de facto protection of legal rights and to access to social services. The EaEU treaty also leaves room for countries to restrict migrants' access to the host labor market in cases "determined by this Treaty and the legislation of the Member States aimed at ensuring their national security (including in economic sectors of strategic importance) and public order" (Article 97.2 of the EaEU treaty). The entry into force of the EaEU comes in parallel with an increasingly securitized migration rhetoric and policy in the Russian Federation and Kazakhstan. In the Russian Federation, the government approved a new regulation according to which migrants are forced to leave the country within five days after two administrative law violations (including traffic fines) or one migration law violation (Schenk 2018), and can be banned from reentering the country for up to 10 years. In this context, challenges remain to enforce the protection of Kyrgyz migrants' rights in the main destination countries, and further collaboration and cooperation with governments are needed. Beyond the EaEU, the Global Compact for Safe, Orderly, and Regular Migration, implemented under the auspices of the United Nations in 2018, presents a framework for comprehensive international cooperation on migrants and human mobility, contributing to the global governance and coordination of international migration policies. The Kyrgyz Republic will highly benefit from signing this treaty, following suit of 164 other countries that have already signed it, in parallel with bilateral agreements reached with main destination countries.

## POSTRETURN

The government of the Kyrgyz Republic should continue supporting temporary migrants at the return stage. During the first semester of the COVID-19 pandemic, the government of the Kyrgyz Republic supported the return of citizens residing abroad who were stranded due to temporary border closures and flight cancellations, facilitating charter flights for Kyrgyz migrants who wanted to return home. By August 24, 2020, 35,469 Kyrgyz citizens had returned from 21 regions of the Russian Federation (Embassy of the Kyrgyz Republic in the Russian Federation 2020b). According to the Ministry of Foreign Affairs and the different consulates, another 5,000 and 2,000 Kyrgyz migrants returned from Türkiye and the United Arab Emirates, respectively, during the same time period. However, many more migrants were still stranded and unable to find a way to return home (King and Zotova 2020). During these uncertain times with different waves of contagion and restrictions, the Kyrgyz Republic should continue to cooperate with the governments of the main receiving countries to facilitate the repatriation of Kyrgyz emigrants who want to return (*Lancet* 2020). Health concerns and limited employment opportunities in receiving countries mean that many migrants may want to return home. Given the dire financial situation of migrants and the spike in the cost of international air transportation, the government should sustain financial assistance for potential returnees and arrange transportation when needed, which could require further coordination with host governments.

Given the particular vulnerabilities of return migrants, especially of those who were forced to return unexpectedly, there is a need to strengthen reintegration plans and services. The concept for the migration policy of the Kyrgyz Republic for 2021–30 recognizes the need to launch reintegration programs for return migrants, although it narrows it to migrants "with negative migration experiences and with a particular focus on women" (State Migration Services 2021).[5] Reintegration programs for return migrants have existed for several years in the Kyrgyz Republic, but they lack a general government strategy and a centralized reintegration mechanism and suffer from very limited resources and outreach. Since the rise in return migration during the COVID-19 pandemic, IOM in the Kyrgyz Republic has worked with local authorities, community leaders, and NGOs to reach returnees, providing them with information and support to access social services, but at a small scale. Kyrgyz returnees would greatly benefit from larger-scale support, such as the ones that are in the process of being implemented in Bangladesh for migrants who returned in the context of COVID-19. Such interventions will deliver services to eligible and interested return migrants to be either sustainably reintegrated into the domestic labor market or to access services to prepare for remigration. The program will also support an upgrade and integration of migration management systems (databases, services, and systems). In order to implement similar interventions in the Kyrgyz Republic, it is essential to develop a comprehensive registry of migrants as recommended in this chapter. Within the broader framework of returnee reintegration, authorities could create a "rapid needs and plans' assessment" form during the registration process at any of the different points of entry (airports, borders), in which, based on returnees' interests and needs, representatives could provide an overview of the services returnees can access, including relevant contact details of service providers (IOM 2019). This information on available support services can help returnees navigate the bureaucratic system. Migration services could reach out to Kyrgyz return migrants to link them to job opportunities through, for example, mediation and job-matching measures, as well as to ensure access to essential services such as health care, shelter, and education.

The large employment losses due to the COVID-19 pandemic and future shocks call for expanding the limited unemployment insurance coverage, in particular to returnees. In the context of the COVID-19 pandemic, unemployment insurance emerged as an essential policy tool to mitigate the welfare impacts of a negative employment shock. In the Kyrgyz Republic, returnees, like other Kyrgyz citizens, have access to unemployment insurance. However, a very small proportion of the unemployed population currently receives unemployment benefits in the Kyrgyz Republic (OECD 2018), and the uptake of unemployment benefits is especially low among return migrants.[6] The low number of registrations originates from a combination of low incentives, strict eligibility criteria, and, more broadly, the limited outreach and capacity of the system. The low monetary unemployment benefits—amounting to between KGS 250 and 500 per month—and short duration—up to six calendar months in a year, but for no more than 12 months over a period of three years—provide limited incentives for returnees to register when compared to the significantly higher earnings' potential abroad. In addition, there are several eligibility criteria, including a minimum frequency of contributions to the social security system of at least 12 months during the last three years and proof of job searching (OECD 2018). As a result, returnees might prefer to wait to migrate again until the conditions for migration improve and mobility restrictions in destination countries have lessened. There is also a limited outreach of this public service, in particular among the vulnerable returnee population, given the strong concentration of centers in urban areas, while migrants tend to come from rural areas. Given all these limitations and the current context of the COVID-19 pandemic, there is an urgent need to expand the reach of the unemployment insurance program and increase the amount of benefits provided, open more centers in rural areas with a high concentration of migrant families, and facilitate its access to vulnerable groups such as returnees, including unemployed returnees, to smooth their income shocks.

Better linkages of return migrants to active labor market policies (ALMPs) are required to support reintegration into home labor markets. While there have been recent legislative and institutional improvements, the variety and reach of ALMPs in the Kyrgyz Republic remain limited. The main ALMPs include public works and small training programs for vulnerable groups, while few resources for other programs for entrepreneurship and self-employment, wage subsidies, job counseling, among others, are available.[7] Overall, these programs are underfunded and use a rather restrictive definition of beneficiaries as, for example, farmers with land plots exceeding 0.05 hectares are considered employed and thus ineligible (World Food Programme, United Nations University UNU-MERIT, and Maastrich Graduate School of Governance 2018).[8] Given the higher prevalence of return migrants in rural areas and the high share who used to work as farmers before migration and engage again in agricultural work upon return—close to half of male return migrants, according to the KIHS (2015)—this policy can de facto limit the ability of return migrants to access ALMPs. The public employment services (PES) provide free training for registered unemployed individuals. However, similarly to unemployment benefits, registration is low, and PES tend to be located and register vacancies in urban areas (Schwegler-Rohmeis, Mummert, and Jarck 2013). As a result, return migrants are very unlikely to use those services.

To better cover return migrants, the endowment to ALMPs should be increased and the eligibility criteria should be relaxed to also include small farmers and provide services in rural areas. Training programs, in particular, could be better linked to employers' demand for skills at destination. In Sri Lanka, for example, the "Skills Passport" was a program introduced by the Tertiary and Vocational Educational Commission (TVEC) of the Ministry of Skills Development, Employment and Labour Relations; the Employers' Federation of Ceylon (EFC); and the International Labour Organization (ILO) and designed to support the successful reintegration of workers returning to Sri Lanka by providing relevant skills and networks with companies (Global Forum on Migration and Development 2020).

Support for entrepreneurial activities may benefit return migrants given their higher rates of self-employment. There are currently no programs in the Kyrgyz Republic that help start self-employment and business ventures.

This void disproportionately affects return migrants, who are overrepresented among the self-employed and entrepreneurs. Thus, interventions to support business startups may provide an essential service to many Kyrgyz returnees.[9] The government recently recognized this need and included in the 2021–30 concept for migration policies the use of "market mechanisms to local entrepreneurs" (State Migration Services 2021). Programs of this sort include a diverse array of services in a "one-stop shop" type of framework where migrants can receive in-kind assistance, financial literacy, support to develop a business plan, and access to banking and microcredit as well as other financial instruments to make productive use of savings. One of the most comprehensive programs of this sort is the Overseas Foreign Worker (OFW) reintegration program provided by the Philippines, which includes training for those who would like to start up small businesses. In order to improve the success rate of entrepreneurial activities, support programs have started to include analyses of skill gaps in local labor markets to ensure that returnees have the skills required and that the entrepreneurial endeavor produces goods or services in high demand in the region of residence (OECD 2020). The IOM in Switzerland has published statistics of success rates of certain business projects in different countries to increase potential returnees' information on home labor markets. More generally, removing administrative and institutional barriers to setting up and running a business can smooth the transition of return migrants to the labor market.

In the longer term, promoting return migration can lead to brain gain and transfer of know-how to the Kyrgyz Republic. One of the guiding principles of the Kyrgyz government's migration agenda is to enhance the attractiveness of returning to the Kyrgyz Republic for the diaspora (State Migration Services 2021). As shown on chapter 1, emigration in the Kyrgyz Republic combines short- and longer-term spells depending on migrants' characteristics. In particular, a sizable part of the Kyrgyz diaspora in the Russian Federation has remained in the country for a long period. These migrants are characterized by relatively higher education levels. The country would benefit from building stronger links with this diaspora by providing more information about employment opportunities in the country and to improve economic conditions in the country to increase the attractiveness of returning for longer-term emigrants, in particular those with higher skills for which there are vacancies in the country. Romania offers one example of engagement with the diaspora through bilateral collaboration between its public employment services (i.e., the Romania Agency for Employment) and that of Italy. Starting in 2009, these two PESs created the MEDIT project with the goal to inform Romanian migrants in Italy about the labor market opportunities in Romania, and cooperate to provide a better institutional support for those migrants who decide to return to Romania (OECD 2013).

Finally, more detailed data collection on returnees in periodic household surveys or in ad hoc surveys is needed to better track their reintegration and design adequate policies. Periodic household surveys need to incorporate questions on return migration in order to better capture the whole extent of the phenomenon and the trends in economic and social outcomes of this group. The Kyrgyz Integrated Household Survey (KIHS) only included questions on returnees in the ad-hoc migration module of 2015, while there is no option to identify returnees in the higher-frequency regular data. Even the 2015 KIHS migration module only captures a small number of return migrants as it asks whether a person residing in the Kyrgyz Republic by the time of the survey had migrated abroad for at least a month during the previous two years. As such, it excludes returnees who had previously returned to the country. Available surveys, with the exception of the 2015 KIHS migration module, do not provide information about the migration journey of return migrants, their human capital accumulation or labor market experience, or the motivations behind the decision to migrate and return (voluntary/involuntary, or planned or unplanned). This lack of information hampers the ability to better understand the impact of migration and to design adequate programs to support migrants throughout their journey, including their reintegration back into the Kyrgyz Republic. Therefore, a longer migration module including the migration history in regular surveys such as the KIHS would be highly beneficial. Furthermore, dedicated ad-hoc surveys administered to return migrants can provide further information on the whole migration history of returnees, shedding further light on the entire life cycle of migration, the interconnectedness of different decisions such as human capital accumulation, entrepreneurship, and savings and migration that could help in implementing better evidence-based policies.

## NOTES

1. For more detail on the G2G between Korea and sending countries, for example, see Cho et al. (2018).
2. Embassy of the Kyrgyz Republic in the Russian Federation (2020a).
3. Decree No. 8446 of the Government of the Russian Federation, June 10, 2020.
4. Resolution No. 4855 of the Government of the Russian Federation, April 12, 2020.
5. Reintegration can be defined as the reintroduction of Kyrgyz emigrants into Kyrgyz society after their migration experience abroad and concerns not only the individual returnee but also communities to which migrants return to (IOM 2018a).
6. According to official statistics from the MLSDM, only 283 returnees registered to obtain unemployment benefits in 2020.
7. The public work program offers employment by public and private employers with wages partially covered by the MLSDM. In 2016, 21,100 people benefited from this program, with an average monthly wage of KGS 1,000-1,5000 (WFP 2018).
8. In 2017, only 1.2 percent of the MLSDM budget was reserved for ALMP (WFP 2018).
9. The effectiveness of entrepreneurship programs for return migrants, however, remains to be rigorously tested (McKenzie and Yang 2015), while existing evidence on the impact of training programs for entrepreneurs in different settings has been rather mixed (McKenzie and Woodruff 2014).

## REFERENCES

Ambler, K., D. Aycinena, and D. Yang. 2014. "Remittance Responses to Temporary Discounts: A Field Experiment among Central American Migrants." NBER Working Paper 20522, September.

Avato, J., J. Koettl, and R. Sabates-Wheeler. 2010. "Social Security Regimes, Global Estimates, and Good Practices: The Status of Social Protection for International Migrants." *World Development* 38 (4): 455–66.

Aycinena, D., C. Martinez, and D. Yang. 2010. "The Impact of Remittance Fees on Remittance Flows: Evidence from a Field Experiment among Salvadoran Migrants." Working paper, University of Michigan.

Azattyk. 2020. "Posol'stvo o pomoshchi migrantam v Rossii: Vydacha deneg ne predusmotrena." [Embassy about help to migrants in Russia: Money transfers are not offered]. April 25. https://rus.azattyk.org/a/30576022.html.

Barsbai, T., V. Licuanan, A. Steinmayr, E. Tiongson, and D. Yang. 2020. "Information and the Acquisition of Social Network Connections." National Bureau of Economic Research Working Paper 27346.

Beam, E. Andrew. 2016. "Do Job Fairs Matter? Experimental Evidence on the Impact of Job-Fair Attendance." *Journal of Development Economics* 120: 32–40.

Cho, Y., A. Denisova, S. Yi, and U. Khadka. 2018. *Bilateral Arrangement of Temporary Labor Migration: Lessons from Korea's Employment Permit System*. Washington, DC: World Bank.

Clemens, M. A. 2015. "Global Skill Partnerships: Proposal for Technical Training in a Mobile World." IZA *Journal of Labor Policy* 4 (2): 1–18.

Doi, Y., D. McKenzie, and B. Zia. 2014. "Who You Train Matters: Identifying Combined Effects of Financial Education on Migrant Households." *Journal of Development Economics* 109 (2): 33–55.

Embassy of the Kyrgyz Republic in the Russian Federation. 2020a. Newsletter "On Temporary Measures to Resolve the Legal Status of Foreign Citizens and Stateless Persons in the Russian Federation in Connection with the Threat of Further Spread of the New Coronavirus Infection (COVID-19). https://mfa.gov.kg/en/dm/Embassy-of-the-Kyrgyz-Republic-in-the-Russian-Federation/news/9491.

Embassy of the Kyrgyz Republic in the Russian Federation. 2020b. "Informatsionnoye soobshcheniye ot 25 avgusta 2020 goda otnositel'no vozvrashcheniya grazhdan Kyrgyzskoy Respubliki iz Rossiyskoy Federatsii." [Informational message from August 25, 2020, regarding return of citizens of the Kyrgyz Republic from the Russian Federation.] August 25. https://mfa.gov.kg/en/dm/posolstvo-kyrgyzskoy-respubliki-v-rossiyskoy-federacii/news/8170.

Eurasian Economic Commission. 2015. "The Treaty on the Eurasian Economic Union Is Effective." January 1. http://www.eurasiancommission.org/en/nae/news/Pages/01-01-2015-1.aspx.

Gibson, J., D. McKenzie, and B. Zia. 2014. "The Impact of Financial Literacy Training for Migrants." *World Bank Economic Review* 28(1): 130–61.

Global Forum on Migration and Development. 2020. "The Future of Human Mobility: Innovative Partnerships for Sustainable Development—Theme 2: Skilling Migrants for Employment." Abu Dhabi, United Arab Emirates.

Gorlin, Y., V. Lyashok, D. Ternovskiy, A. Bozhechkova, P. Trunin, S. Zubov, A. Kaukin, and E. Miller. 2020. "Monitoring the Economic Situation in Russia: Trends and Challenges of Socio-Economic Development." Institute for Economic Policy, Russian akademyma of the National Economy and Public Service under the President of the Russian Federation.

Honorati, M., S. Yi, and T. Choi. 2020. "Assessing the Vulnerability of Armenian Temporary Labor Migrants during the COVID-19 Pandemic." Social Protection and Jobs Discussion Paper 2003. World Bank, Washington, DC.

ILO (International Labour Organization). 2013. "Pre-Departure Training Programme, Republic of the Philippines." http://www.ilo.org/dyn/migpractice/migmain.showPractice?p_lang=en&p_practice_id=72.

IOM (International Organization for Migration). 2011. "IOM Migrant Training Programmes Overview, 2010–2011." http://www.iom.int/jahia/webdav/shared/shared/mainsite/activities/facilitating/IOM_Migrant_Training_Programmes_Overview_2010_2011.pdf.

IOM (International Organization for Migration). 2018a. "Enhancing Migrant Well-Being Upon Return Through an Integrated Approach to Reintegration." Global Compact Thematic Paper, Reintegration.

IOM (International Organization for Migration). 2018b. "Supporting Safe, Orderly and Dignified Migration Through Assisted Voluntary Return and Reintegration." Global Compact Thematic Paper, Assisted Voluntary Return and Reintegration.

IOM (International Organization for Migration). 2019. "Reintegration Handbook: Practical Guidance on the Design, Implementation and Monitoring of Reintegration Assistance." International Organization for Migration, Geneva.

IOM (International Organization for Migration) and UNICEF. 2020. "Rapid Needs Assessment of the Challenges Facing Migrant Workers and Their Families Impacted by the Covid-19 Outbreak." A study based on the surveys of Kyrgyz labor migrants and members of their families left behind and NGO representatives.

Jenish, N. 2013. "Business Cycles in Central Asia and the Russian Federation." University of Central Asia, Institute of Public Policy and Administration Working Paper 15.

Karymshakov, K., and B. Sulaimanova. 2017. "Migration Impact on Left-Behind Women's Labour Participation and Time-Use: Evidence from Kyrgyzstan." UNU-WIDER Working Paper 119. Helsinki: United Nations University World Institute for Development Economic Research.

King, E., and N. Zotova. 2020 "Situational Brief: COVID-19 and Associated Risks for Central Asian Temporary Labour Migrants in the Russian Federation." migrationhealth.org. https://1bec58c3-8dcb-46b0-bb2afd4addf0b29a.filesusr.com/ugd/188e74_953c1267139844a3a0708261b858e455.pdf.

Kroeger, A., and K. H. Anderson. 2014. "Remittances and the Human Capital of Children: New Evidence from Kyrgyzstan During Revolution and Financial Crisis, 2005–2009." *Journal of Comparative Economics* 42: 777–85.

Kuznetsova, I, R. Mogilevskii, A. Murzakulova, A. Abdoubaetova, A. Wolters, and J. Round. 2020. "Migration and COVID-19: Challenges and Policy Responses in the Kyrgyz Republic." CAP paper 247 (December), Central Asia Program.

*Lancet.* 2020. "Leaving No One Behind in the Covid-19 Pandemic: A Call for Urgent Global Action to Include Migrants & Refugees in the Covid-19 Response." April 10, *Lancet* Migration. https://www.migrationandhealth.org/statements.

Lokshin, M., and E. Glinskaya. 2009. "The Effect of Male Migration on Employment Patterns of Women in Nepal." *World Bank Economic Review* 23 (3): 481–507.

Madiyev, O. 2021. "The Eurasian Economic Union: Repaving Central Asia's Road to Russia?" Migration Policy Institute, February 11. https://www.migrationpolicy.org/article/eurasian-economic-union-central-asia-russia.

Martin, R., and D. Radu. 2012. "Return Migration: The Experience of Eastern Europe." *International Migration* 50 (6): 109–28.

McKenzie, D., J. Gibson, and S. Stillman. 2013. "A Land of Milk and Honey with Streets Paved with Gold: Do Emigrants Have Over-Optimistic Expectations About Incomes Abroad?" *Journal of Development Economics* 102: 116–27.

McKenzie, D., and C. Woodruff. 2014. "What Are We Learning from Business Training Evaluations Around the Developing World?" *World Bank Research Observer* 29 (1): 48–82.

McKenzie, D., and D. Yang. 2015. "Evidence on Policies to Increase the Development Impact of International Migration." *World Bank Research Observer* 30 (2): 155–92.

Moroz, Harry, Maheshwor Shrestha, and Mauro Testaverde. 2020. "Potential Responses to the COVID-19 Outbreak in Support of Migrant Workers."

OECD (Organisation for Economic Co-operation and Development). 2018. "Social Protection System Review of Kyrgyzstan." OECD Development Pathways, OECD Publishing, Paris. https://www.oecd.org/countries/kyrgyzstan/Social_Protection_System_Review_Kyrgyzstan.pdf.

OECD (Organisation for Economic Co-operation and Development). 2020. "Supporting Sustainable Reintegration." In *Sustainable Reintegration of Return Migrants: A Better Homecoming.* Paris: OECD Publishing. https://doi.org/10.1787/5fee55b3-en.

Ryazantsev, S., and M. Khramova. 2020. "Influence of the COVID-19 Pandemic on the Position of Migrants and Remittances in Central Asia." Institute for Socio-Political Research of the Russian Academy of Sciences.

Schenk, C. 2018. "Labour Migration in the Eurasian Economic Union." In *Migration and the Ukraine Crisis: A Two-Country Perspective*, edited by Agnieszka Pikulicka-Wilczewska and Greta Uehling. London: E-International Relations.

Schwegler-Rohmeis, W., A. Mummert, and K. Jarck. 2013. "Labour Market and Employment Policy in the Kyrgyz Republic: Identifying Constraints and Options for Employment

Development." Deutsche Gesellschaft für Internationale Zusammenarbeit (GIZ) GmbH, Eschborn/Bishkek, Germany.

Shrestha, M. 2020. "Get Rich or Die Tryin': Perceived Earnings, Perceived Mortality Rates, and Migration Decisions of Potential Work Migrants from Nepal." *World Bank Economic Review* 34 (1): 1–27.

Shrestha, M., A. M. Mobarak, and I. A. Sharif. 2019. "Migration and Remittances: The Impacts of a Government Intermediated International Migration Program." World Bank, Washington, DC.

State Migration Services. 2021. "Concept for the Migration Policy of the Kyrgyz Republic for 2021–2030." Government of the Kyrgyz Republic.

Testaverde, M., H. Moroz, C. H. Hollweg, and A. Schmillen. 2017. "Migrating to Opportunity: Overcoming Barriers to Labor Mobility in Southeast Asia." World Bank, Washington, DC. https://openknowledge.worldbank.org/handle/10986/28342.

Vershaver, E., N. Ivanova, and A. Rocheva. 2020. "Migrants in Russia during the COVID-19 Pandemic: Survey Results." https://papers.ssrn.com/sol3/papers.cfm?abstract_id=3672397.

World Bank. 2016. "Systematic Country Diagnostic for Eight Small Pacific Island Countries: Priorities for Ending Poverty and Boosting Shared Prosperity." Washington, DC, World Bank. https://openknowledge.worldbank.org/handle/10986/23952.

World Food Programme, United Nations University UNU-MERIT, and Maastrich Graduate School of Governance. 2018. "Scoping Study on Social Protection and Safety Nets for Enhanced Food Security and Nutrition in the Kyrgyz Republic." World Food Programme, Rome.